CITIZEN PAUL

Books by Ralph Schoenstein

The Block

Time Lurches On

With T-Shirts and Beer Mugs for All

My Year in the White House Doghouse

Little Spiro

I Hear America Mating

Wasted on the Young

Yes, My Darling Daughters

Citizen Paul

CITIZEN PAUL

A STORY OF FATHER & SON

Ralph Schoenstein

FARRAR STRAUS GIROUX

NEW YORK

A portion of this book appeared,
in somewhat different form, in *New York*

Library of Congress Cataloging in Publication Data
Schoenstein, Ralph.   Citizen Paul.
1. Schoenstein, Paul. 2. Schoenstein, Ralph.
3. Journalists—United States—Biography. I. Title.
PN4874.S333S3   070'.92'4 [B]   78-17986

For

his Mimi

and

his Carol

CONTENTS

CITIZEN PAUL

1

CITIZEN RALPH

"And, Johnny, what does *your* father do?"
"He plays piano in a whorehouse, teacher."
"Johnny, how can you *say* such a terrible thing!"
"Teacher, how can I say he works for Hearst?"
—Ancient journalism joke

My father never played piano in a whorehouse, but there were many times when I wanted him to audition. Although I was happy as a boy, I lived under a cloud that also must have rained on a girl named Patricia Hearst.

It was an afternoon in early May of 1944, in a public school on the West Side of New York, when I first discovered that my father was a noted war criminal. On that unforgettable afternoon, I was slouching dreamily at my desk in Mrs. Sondra Krim's history class, a boy of almost eleven, who was uncertain about the nature of whorehouses and Hearst, but who could draw profiles of Japanese fighter planes and Jane Russell's breasts.

Across the aisle from me was my friend Freddie Cohen, who could blow bubbles with his tongue and who now was explaining to Mrs. Krim why Eleanor Roosevelt was a Communist.

3

"Who told you such *absolute rubbish?*" said the horrified woman, who had been in the Spanish Civil War with the Abraham Lincoln Brigade.

"Fulton Lewis Junior," Freddie replied, turning to smile at me.

"Fulton Lewis *Junior?*" she said with a blend of outrage and incredulity. "Frederic, you actually *listen* to Fulton Lewis *Junior?*"

"Sure," said Freddie. "He comes on before the Lone Ranger."

Since I also made the same radio trip from the ultra right to the conquest of wrong, I suddenly found myself saying, "Mrs. Krim, I hear Fulton Lewis Junior, too."

"Ralph, an *A* student like *you* listens to that *trash?*" she said, as if I had declared myself a fan of Axis Sally.

"Oh, I don't need any Eleanor Roosevelt stuff," I said. "I get all the news from my father, sometimes even before it happens."

"Really? What does your father do?"

I smiled and then I said as if taking the oath for the Presidency, "He's the City Editor of the *New York Journal-American.*"

I knew, of course, that unless a boy's father happened to play for the Yankees, editor of the whole city was the most exalted job to be had; and so I was stunned by the pain on Mrs. Krim's face as she said accusingly, "Ralph, your father works for *Hearst?*"

"Gee, I'm not sure," I said. "I'll have to ask him."

"The *Journal-American* is one of William Randolph Hearst's yellow journals."

Her words were like a body blow, for in 1944 only the Japanese were yellow. That year it was not the color to be.

"I . . . didn't know that," I said, embarrassed by the snickers in the class. "I know it's an American paper for the American people."

To counteract her use of yellow, I had quoted the red-white-and-blue declaration that appeared on the masthead of the paper every day.

"Hearst and the *Journal-American* started the Spanish-American War," she said. "And, class, we know what the Spanish-American War was, don't we?"

"Oh, *yes*," they sang, the little finks.

"Ralph, I'm sure that your father is a very lovely man," said Mrs. Krim, "but if he has to work for a newspaper, it's really too bad that he's not with the *Times*."

"But my father . . . well, he's done some *terrific things*," I said, upset by the view of his empty pedestal. "He just exposed a big *gambling* ring. They arrested two hundred guys in one night because of what he told the D.A. I mean, he had reporters pretending to be *crooks*—well, not exactly *crooks*, but not reporters either."

Throughout my impassioned though garbled defense of my father, Mrs. Krim held her somber look. She obviously felt that breaking up a blackjack game was insufficient atonement for having started a war that I vaguely remembered had come between Civil and I.

"Thank you for telling us all that, Ralph," she said. "All right, children, we will talk more about Mr. Hearst when we come to our lesson on famous warmongers."

The moment the bell sounded at the end of history class, the other boys descended on me to take a look at my scarlet H.

"So your old man started the Spanish-American War," Beanie Meyerhoffer said.

"Fuck you, Beanie," I glibly replied.

"Hey, how'd your father do that?" said Maurey DuBoff. "He attack Spain or somethin'?"

"It wasn't my *father,* you jackasses," I said. "It was a guy named *Hearst.* My father never even *met* him."

"That ain't what Mrs. *Krim* thinks and she's the *teacher,*" Beanie said. "You better get a new father or you're gonna flunk."

A few minutes later, when I got home, I went to the *Encyclopaedia Britannica,* looked up the Spanish-American War, and felt a blessed moment of relief. What absolute *morons* all of them were: that war had been fought in 1898, four years before my father was *born.* The book did mention the nudge that Hearst had given hostilities; but the Spanish had been attacked by—of *all* people—Eleanor Roosevelt's uncle, Teddy. I wondered if Mrs. Krim knew that there was a warmonger in her favorite family! I would have to hit her with this black sheep the next time she tried to make my father sound like Admiral Yamamoto.

At dinner that night, after my father had twice interrupted his meal to take calls from the *Journal-American,* I looked at him uneasily and said, "You know what my history teacher told me today?"

"You mean the one who's a Commie?" he said as he wiped up some gravy with a piece of bread that he had torn from the end of a loaf.

"You shouldn't call her that," my mother said. "She's not a Communist. She's a liberal who fought in Spain."

"Is that where she got the hole in her head?" my father said, and we both laughed.

"Well, what she said," I told him, "is that you started the Spanish-American War."

"Jesus, *that* one again." And then he smiled. "Tell her I'm innocent. And I also didn't kill Christ."

"Maybe you could give him a note," my mother said.

"Right. 'Dear Mrs. Lenin. Please excuse my son from guilt by association with his father's boss.' Remind me to spit in that woman's eye on the next open school night."

"I know all about the war," I told him. "I just looked it up. But you better tell me if you started *anything* that I should know about 'cause Mrs. Krim got the kids all worked up."

"Well, Poop," he said, "I run the city desk—that filthy room you like to play in—and we don't get much chance to cook up wars. But I'm afraid you're kind of stuck with that Spanish-American stuff because Mr. Hearst was involved in it and we're a Hearst newspaper—the flagship, in fact."

"But you're against the Japs and Germans—aren't you?"

"Oh, harder than anyone," he said. "MacArthur is fight-

ing especially for *us*. You see, the Hearst papers *are* color-
ful, but that's not a crime. A headline isn't wrong because
it's red instead of black. And believe it or not, the *Journal*
is often much better on a story than the holy *Times*."

"Better than the *Times?*" I said in disbelief.

"Absolutely. There are some stories that the *Times* just
doesn't know how to cover."

"Listen, I gotta *know*. Tell me some good things for the
Journal and some stinkin' things for the *Times!*"

As he began giving part of a talk that he had given at
the Columbia School of Journalism, I grabbed a pencil and
pad, eager for the ammunition to counterattack those who
had mocked the greatest father in New York, a title he
held in spite of strong competition. Freddie's father sold
insurance and knew when people would drop dead; Max's
father owned a building and could throw people out into
the street; and Beanie's father had been in the Navy and
once had bumped into a whale.

"First of all, the *Times* has its share of prejudices," my
father said, "and it often judges the news—like local crime
stories it considers too shocking for the horsey set."

No crime for horsey set, I wrote on the pad.

"It also makes plenty of mistakes, but it makes them
with dignity."

Dignified mistakes, I wrote.

"And it's also badly edited because the stories are much
too long and the makeup makes no attempt to draw the
reader in. The *News* and *Mirror* are much better edited,
and of course the *Journal* is, too."

Not edited, I wrote.

"The *Times* is just too aloof; it isn't interested in cover-
ing New York City," he said, for those were the days when
that newspaper's metropolitan coverage embodied all the
drama of chess matches, stock issues, and docking ships.
"A plane's gotta hit the Empire State before they really
come alive."

He and I would be joining the *Times* in coming alive
the following summer, when an Army bomber lost in
a fog made that very connection with the Empire State
Building while my father was touring my camp in Ver-
mont, pretending to enjoy the activities while looking
around for a bottle of gin. After hearing the news from
someone with a portable radio, my father and I had
run down a country road to a general store, where he
had commandeered a phone and directed the *Journal-
American's* moves while perched on a Dr. Pepper box. In
between deep sucks of smoke, he took possession of the
story with a litany I loved:

"I want good follow-ups with all the families from the
New York area . . . and tell Ray a page of pictures for
two or three—all the stuff you've got from inside the building . . . and an architect's rendition, too, with a drawing
of how the plane came in . . . and tell Creamer I want a
solid piece about the kind of plane it was—was it the kind
from Doolittle's raid?—and have his Army connections explain exactly why the damn thing was so low and if it
could ever happen again. How many of these things fly
over New York? I want that *run,* no matter how he has to

get it . . . and of course good Dewey and La Guardia quotes . . . and punch up every eyewitness story you can get—send Collins and Hoffman and Judy over there—and have one of 'em go to the observation tower and . . ."

And jump off, he might have said, to get the pilot's view of things, for there was always something original about the way he brought the news to the people who swept the stables for the horsey set.

As I sat beside him in that store, I tried to help him by drawing an Army bomber hitting the Empire State; but my father needed no help. He had taken over that building like a journalistic King Kong.

"Okay, now give me some more good stuff for the *Journal*'s side," I said as we sat at dinner a year before the crash, when he had first begun to tarnish the *Times*.

He lit a cigarette and started reviewing some of his triumphs since becoming City Editor of the *Journal-American* in 1938. My favorite was his exposé of conditions at a mental hospital named Rockland State by having a reporter fake insanity and get himself committed there; and my father's even greater achievement had been in getting the reporter out after a board of psychiatrists had given his performance a rave review.

Now that my father's triumphs were ready for flaunting at my friends, I tried to make my counterattack even stronger by going back to the books in search of virtues for William Randolph Hearst. Finding them was more challenging than trigonometry homework because Hearst hadn't thought of too many things since thinking up the

Spanish-American War. In fact, in those almost fifty years since 1898, he had managed not to utter a single memorable line, a stunning accomplishment for the Editor-in-Chief of the biggest publishing empire on earth. At last, however, I discovered that he had suggested free milk for the infants of the poor and also opposed the use of dogs for surgical experiments. Such multi-species compassion could not have come from a Genghis Khan, so I happily made a few more notes.

Putting the encyclopedia aside, I then made a slow and careful review of the day's edition of *The New York Times* and was elated to find two mistakes: the weather forecast of a cloudless night already dramatically wrong: a thunderstorm had just begun; and a baseball writer had spelled the first name of Yankee pitcher Chandler as "Sturgeon." His correct name, of course, was Spurgeon, always written that way in the *Journal,* where no one ever called him a fish.

About an hour later, while my father and I were listening to the "Kraft Music Hall," my cousin Sam phoned me and I proudly described all of my research. He replied by giving me my first hearing of the pianist-in-a-whorehouse joke and I was suddenly in despair, for now I knew that my scarlet H was no mere junior-varsity letter. I would have to fight like a Roosevelt if I wanted to see it disappear.

The following day, my great effort began. Glowing with authority, I marched through the schoolyard, found Beanie, and said, "So you think the holy *New York Times* is so *great?* Well, how'd you like to know that they just got

the *weather* wrong and they can't even spell Spud Chandler's *name!*"

"Yeah, but they don't work for Hearst," he replied.

"Oh, *yeah?*" I said.

He either had me or was being idiotic. I couldn't think
fast enough to figure it out.

"You just better hope that Carlos don't find out about
that Spanish war your old man started or he'll put another
crack in your ass," Beanie said.

"What a *moron* you are!" I cried. "Do you know who
fought in Spain? Mrs. *Krim herself, that's* who!"

Since the Spanish-American War was fought four thousand miles from Spain, I now was sounding as grandly nit-
witty as a Hearst editorial that urged Congressional support for Mother's Day. My lack of logic didn't sink me,
however, because Beanie's train of thought had even more
uncouplings than my own.

"Mrs. Krim fought for *Abraham Lincoln*," he said. "And
besides, she didn't *start* it like your old man. She was just
a WAAC or somethin'."

"Oh, *yeah?* Well, how'd you like to know that my father
put a guy in an *insane* asylum just to get a story! The
shitty *Times* didn't do it. They were too busy getting Spud
Chandler's *name* wrong!"

"Those Hearst guys *belong* in nut houses," Beanie said
with a maddening smirk; and that was when I jumped
him.

The fight was a little shorter than the Spanish-American

War. Beanie simply removed my arms from his neck and hit me once in the mouth.

As I walked home from school that day, my tongue kept tasting the split in my lip and I wished that my father had *been* on the *Times,* no matter how defective their spelling and barometer were. Dammit, why had I gone into battle with the insane-asylum story instead of telling Beanie how Eleanor Roosevelt had recently praised the Hearst Milk Fund! He might have just settled for twisting my arm.

When I reached my apartment house, a building on 78th Street between Amsterdam Avenue and Broadway, I saw my father waving to a couple of men in a car that was pulling away from the curb.

"Hi-ya, Poop," I said.

"Hey, what happened to *you?*" he said, seeing my lip.

"Just a stickball game. I hit a lamppost going after a fly."

"We'd better have your mother put something on that right away."

"Who were those guys in the car?"

"Believe it or not," he said, "they're with the F.B.I."

"The *F.B.I.?*" I cried. "No *kidding!* And they're pals of *yours?*"

"Well, sort of."

Nobody's father knew agents of the F.B.I., whose program was three after Fulton Lewis Junior.

My father then told me that one of his reporters had discovered a German spy who was living at the Taft Hotel, the very place where my cousin Herbie was unsuspectingly planning to have his bar-mitzvah lunch in two weeks. My father had given this story to the F.B.I. an hour before he printed it, so that the paper would have its scoop but not alert the agent and thus spoil the arrest. The F.B.I., however, had also wanted to know how my father had been able to play counterspy at the Taft.

"And you won't tell them?" I said.

"A newspaperman never reveals his sources," he replied. "It's journalism's cardinal sin."

"The First Amendment!" I said, as if impressing Mrs. Krim.

"Yes, I learned all about the First Amendment at Harvard," he said in the voice he always used to make fun of higher education. "It was one of Father's favorites."

My father didn't know the Ten Amendments from the Seven Dwarfs: he simply knew you protected informants, something he may have known when he began selling papers on the streets of Harlem at the age of twelve; and so, for the past few days, these two federal agents had been following him home, driving out of radio fantasy and into our stickball field. It was as intoxicating as if the Green Hornet had been seen on the corner eating bagels and lox.

"I've started saying goodbye to them," said my father, a chicken who had been pausing to charm the fox. "I guess you could say that we've become friends."

"Friends with the *F.B.I.*—while they're *chasing* you—

boy, that's *terrific!*" I cried, savoring my victory. "Just wait'll I tell those bastards at school!"

"No," my father said. "I want you to keep this one a secret."

"I won't reveal the source," I said; and then I realized in dismay that the source and the subject of this story were one. I couldn't say that the F.B.I. had been following my doorman home.

The next morning at school, I cornered Beanie, Freddie, and Maurey, smiled enigmatically, and said, "What I could tell you if I could."

No one seemed to know what the hell I was talking about; if they had known, there might have been a battle over the scoring of the deeds of Paul Schoenstein and William Randolph Hearst. If a war with Spain was demerits and milk for hungry babies was points, what was catching a German spy without telling your country how you knew where he was? Points, I finally decided—the Lone Ranger always worked that way—and so I was maddened by the frustration of not being able to counterattack with this incredibly heroic tale.

In the days that followed, I lost heart for the fight. From time to time, I would brandish a *Times* that had typographical mistakes, but these were small, joyless victories. As if now sensing my defeat, Mrs. Krim stopped accusing my father of leading America into war and she stopped suggesting that he apply for honest employment at the *Times;* and the boys stopped mocking me as well, either out of pity for a fallen foe or because they'd forgotten which side they were on. Dennis Feeney, for example, took a notable turn to the right when he praised the work that Father Coughlin had been doing at Boys Town; but I didn't pounce on his mistake and explain that he had confused a Fascist priest with Father Flanagan. Why use a cherry bomb when I couldn't drop my blockbuster on him: curbside cordiality with the F.B.I. And therefore, resisting such tempting encounters, I had to pass each day with a grimly silent pride in my father's work, in his counterfeit lunatics, captured spies, contented babies, and federal friends. I probably would have managed to keep on losing anyway, for Beanie and Maurey would have said, "Well, the *Times* doesn't *have* to be trained by the feds because it's part of the *government!*" My scarlet H would still have been there.

And then, like a miracle, it happened. One afternoon I came home from school and found my mother jubilant.

"The most wonderful thing has happened!" she said. "Your father just won the Pulitzer Prize!"

"Terrific!" I said. "What is it?"

"A prize from Columbia University for the best reporting of the year. It's a very great honor and no Hearst editor has *ever* gotten one."

"Is it a secret?"

"Oh no, it'll be in all the papers."

"Even the *Times?*"

"On the front page."

"By God, I've got 'em, I've *got* 'em!" I cried, ecstatic at finding myself in possession of the ultimate weapon. "I've really got 'em now!"

My mother then told me why my father had received the Pulitzer Prize: for reporting a supremely dramatic event that he conveniently had staged himself. He had saved the life of a dying child in New York named Patricia Malone by procuring a new drug that my mother pronounced pee-ni-cillin. Patricia's father had called my father to say that she was suffering from a fierce blood disease and had just seven hours to live unless she was given penicillin, a word unknown to Americans in the summer of 1943. There was none of it at her hospital because the nation's tiny supply belonged to the Army Medical Corps. At once, my father called the Surgeon General and talked him into releasing some penicillin for Patricia Malone; and then a *Journal* radio car, escorted by New Jersey State Police, rushed the drug from the Squibb factory in New Brunswick to the Lutheran Hospital in New York, beating death by less than three hours. If Patricia's father had called the *Times*, he would have been referred to the A.M.A.

When my mother had finished her splendid story, I ran out of the house and down to the street to engage the enemy again. I found them sitting on the steps of a brownstone, where I tried to be casual while I said, "Anyone happen to know what a Pulitzer Prize is?"

"Sure," said Maurey. "It's a terrific thing. It comes from the King of Sweden."

"Well, my father just won one," I said.

"*Sure* he did."

"The king just called my *mother.*"

"*Sure* he did."

"You wanna make a little bet, like maybe a million dollars?" I said. "Just read tomorrow's *Times.*"

"Your father really *won* one?" Dennis said. "Hey, that's fantastic. What for?"

"He discovered peenice-illin." I sounded as if I were describing a new genital disease.

"What the hell is that?" Beanie said.

"A new sulfa drug," I replied.

"And he *discovered* it?"

"Well, he didn't *completely* discover it, but he's gonna make it something really big."

Beanie looked at me with suspicion, but without the brains to wonder if penicillin might not have caught on all by itself. For three or four seconds, he strained for a comeback and then he said, "Your father ain't no druggist."

"Look, Beanie," I said with grand condescension, "you'll just have to read tomorrow's *Times* or listen to Fulton Lewis Junior."

"Any dough with it?" said Freddie. "Or just a cup?"

"Gee, I don't know," I said. "Anybody know the answer to that?" I was willing to lead a discussion of the prize for another hour or two.

"Oh, there's dough with it," said Maurey. "From an old millionaire who makes dynamite."

"*Dynamite,*" said Beanie. "Sure, it figures. That's why

it's a prize for guys who start wars. The good old Spanish-American."

"Beanie, you're the king of the schmucks," Dennis said. "His father didn't get the prize for starting the Spanish-American *War*."

"Yeah, but they musta known about it and it didn't hurt."

Beanie and Maurey then began a seminar about the effect of the Spanish-American War on the Pulitzer Prize, with Freddie and Dennis contributing all the misinformation at their command. It was hard for me to hear everything they said because I was busy listening to the sound of a certain piano fading away.

2

HELLO, MISTER NEW YORK

On a Saturday morning in May of 1946, a rabbi named Neumann addressed a congregation on the West Side of New York and condemned a bar mitzvah that had been held the week before. The bar mitzvah had been mine, and Neumann's was the only bad review, for Walter Winchell, Dorothy Kilgallen, and Ed Sullivan had given it raves.

Why had Rabbi Neumann been moved to pan my coming of age? Because my cantor had been off-key? Because my Torah had been a paperback? No, he had panned it because it had been staged by Paul Schoenstein with a style more appropriate for the opening of a bridge. My father did everything with an elegant excess that he called "traveling first-class." He was a man who enjoyed overpaying for clothes at stores that catered to self-made aristocrats; and so he felt that the God of Abraham rated the Perroquet Suite of the Waldorf-Astoria, where a ninety-pound boy of thirteen made a welcoming speech to two mayors, three comedians, four judges, a dozen columnists, a ballroom-dance team, a cabaret singer, a promising middleweight, a recording engineer, two dozen relatives, and three hundred friends. It was a bar mitzvah that could have been packaged for prime time and called Stars Over Israel.

There was comedy, music, and sex all at once when a sultry young blonde named Penny Edwards began to fondle my pompadour while singing a song rich with double entendre entitled "He's a Big Boy Now." One entendre, however, was wasted because I was so small that I looked like a Munchkin in a business suit and I was in a better position to arouse her kneecaps than her breasts.

When the song was over, my father, anesthetized by toasts to my maturity, walked up to the microphone with a great silly smile and replaced me as Penny Edwards's flame.

"Put your arm around me, honey," he said to her; and then he tried to sing "Embraceable You," but he lacked a certain command of the words.

"Embrace me . . . you . . . Embrace me . . . Replace me," he sang with a wingéd heart and a heavy tongue; and he probably would have said "Deface me" had Penny not started to give him the words with a glee that revealed her awareness of what it meant to be molested by the City Editor of the country's biggest evening paper.

"You're sweet, honey . . . Keep your arm there . . . Embrace me . . . Embrace me . . . you sweet untraceable you . . . You're terrific, honey . . . Call me at Cortland 7–2762 . . . Hey, Ralph, see how it's done?" he said while I sat embarrassed on the dais beside a friend named Ronnie who said with a reverence befitting a bar-mitzvah day, "Hey, I think your old man's gettin' tit."

It was perhaps this mixture of theology and tit that moved Rabbi Neumann to view my bar mitzvah as the kind of Jewish event that strengthened Christianity. He was upset by all the celebrities at my Judaeo-pagan rites, but each of them was my father's friend; and none was more treasured than Jimmy Walker, the song writer who had also been a Mayor of New York, the man who'd been driven from office by a commission that found no music in the corruption over which he unknowingly reigned.

"Ralph, following you today is harder than following William Jennings Bryan," said Walker in his rich and polished voice while two of my aunts sighed noisily and Leonard Lyons began to write an item to appear in the *New York Post*. "You know, since the day when my two children went to see the circus with you, I have looked upon you with affectionate interest. But this morning . . . Ralph, this morning when I saw you embrace that Torah, I felt such a thrill and such pride in you. And now I'll tell you a little secret. Ralph, there was a goy in that temple today."

He could have been referring to my father, who spent less time in temples than the average archbishop. My father and Walker were more at home at a corner table in Toots Shor's, where I sometimes ate with them on Friday nights before we went to Madison Square Garden to see Henry Armstrong, Rocky Graziano, Gus Lesnevich,

Willie Pep, Sugar Ray Robinson, or Beau Jack. I was the only child who ever sat with the ringside working press, where my father loved to hold court, greeting dozens of men with an easy smile, a musical *"Hey,"* and then some conversational vamping while looking for the next old friend to hail. With a flair for insincerity that could have carried him to the White House had he not been Jewish, my father often seemed to be running for President of Madison Square Garden, although he already held a higher post.

"You know, your old man is Mister New York," he told me one night before we saw LaMotta take on Sugar Ray. "That guy who just came over—Jim Farley—he made Roosevelt and I know him better than I know you."

He said these same words so many times: he knew hundreds of people better than he knew me. Had I taken him literally, I would have stood in his world somewhere between the Fire Commissioner and the doorman at "21"; but by the time I was twelve, I knew that my father, like his friend Jimmy Walker, had a talent for converting bullshit into hyperbolic charm.

"You weren't really listening to Farley: you kept using non sequiturs," I told him, using a word I had just learned at school.

"Aw, he's as phony as a three-dollar bill," my father said, "but he's a helluva guy."

"But that doesn't make any *sense,*" I said. "I mean, it's contradictory to say that he's as phony as—"

"Hey, *Tom!*" he suddenly called to the Governor of New York, who stopped and said through a mouth that barely moved, "Hello, Paul. Nice to see you again." Thomas E. Dewey was as cold as my father was warm, but they were both good baritones who once sang a duet at the Legislative Correspondents Dinner in Albany, where I was again the token child. My father had never said that he knew Tom Dewey better than he knew me, but I think he knew him better than he knew my sister; and while they stood in the aisle and talked, I wondered if Dewey was a higher or lower denomination of phony than Farley.

"Is *he* as phony as a three-dollar bill?" I said when Dewey moved away.

"No, he's a helluva guy and a terrific executive," said my father, who might have made the same remark after having a laugh with Attila the Hun. "And did you hear how he talked to your old man?"

"Yeah, that was great. Did you really help him break Murder Incorporated?"

"I didn't do him any harm. You know, for a guy who never made it to high school, your old man has done pretty well. In fact, I sort of run this town."

Because it was hard to disbelieve anything my father ever said in his direct and disarming style, I did believe he was Mister New York, especially on that Saturday at the Waldorf-Astoria, when the man who helped him run the city, Mayor William O'Dwyer, walked up to the microphone and apologized for being late.

"I was stuck at City Hall settling a tugboat strike," he said. "You could have settled it faster, Paul. Those sailors would rather deal with one of their own."

O'Dwyer knew that my father had once been an able-bodied seaman, the most literate sixth-grade dropout ever to sail the Luckenbach Line.

For the next few minutes, the Mayor of New York discussed his adviser, Paul Schoenstein, and my pride in my father's tugboat-strike-settling potential made me even more unbearable than I had been in my pompously squeaky synagogue speech.

"How many mayors did *your* bar mitzvah get?" I asked my friend Ronnie as we sat on the dais. I sounded as if I were collecting baseball cards.

"Well, I had the head of Bloomingdale's," he said.

"And that's your best shot? Listen, you know what I call O'Dwyer? I call him *Uncle Bill.*"

"And you know what my *father* calls him? A crook. He says that Walker was crooked, too. Doesn't your old man know any *honest* mayors?"

"Of *course* he does," I said. "I went to the rodeo with La Guardia, didn't I?"

"And something's gonna come out on him—you just watch."

After the party had ended, I asked my father if Bill O'Dwyer and Jimmy Walker were honest men, for Walker had been driven into exile to Europe and O'Dwyer was becoming the subject of suspicions that would heighten when he left America too.

"Of *course* they're honest men," he said. "They're both sweet guys." And then, while I tried to unscramble this offbeat theory of criminology, he gave me his boyish smile and said, "Your mother's uncle, the judge—now *there* was a crook. The bastard would take a red-hot stove."

I never knew my maternal grand-uncle, the man who collected glowing stoves, but I knew Walker and O'Dwyer and saw the affection they felt for the editor who informally handled their public relations. If a person had any potential for sweetness, my father was able to waken it. O'Dwyer, a cool and colorless man who managed to be Irish while having no charm, was roused to minimal merriness by my father, whom he often called to discuss a decision he was planning to make; and on many nights when I wanted to sit with my father and hear Ish Kabibble or Baby Snooks, he and my mother were summoned to Gracie Mansion to be companions for Uncle Bill.

"The poor guy has been so lonely since Kathleen died," my father told me one night when I wanted to settle by the radio with him.

"But do you have to go there so *often?*" I said.

"Your father is Uncle Bill's baby-sitter," said my mother with an edge. "And then he'll be up at five-thirty tomorrow to unlock the *Journal,* won't you, dear?"

"I'm not going to tell you again," he told her as a fear of his anger took hold of me. "I *have* to get down there by seven to read all the columns before the news starts to break. For Crissake, how many times do I have to *say* it? I'm a slow *reader*—you should *know* that by now."

"Sure, *I* understand that," I eagerly said. "And I understand why you're going tonight."

I would have understood relativity if it could have kept my father's temper in check.

"Poop," he said to me warmly, "Uncle Bill is alone and that's something we have never been. You don't know how lucky we are to have the family we do."

My father's feeling for his family was passionate every day of his life, from the time when he dumped the first money he earned directly into his mother's lap, through the years when he welcomed my mother's parents at his table every night, to the time when he told me, "It would be wonderful if all of us lived together in one big house." On July 2, 1961, my wife and I and our new baby joined my sister, her husband, her child, and my parents in a big house in the country, where my father's dream of a cock-eyed commune at last became reality. On July 6, I hit my brother-in-law in the face with a profoundly sincere right cross that upset my father, even though it was the closest he had gotten to a Friday-night fight in years.

I did better with my Irish-Catholic relatives like Uncle Bill. One Sunday morning in early September of 1949, I was sitting on the porch of Gracie Mansion, being less than spellbound by a conversation about the wages of garbage men, when O'Dwyer said that he was going to Syracuse next week for a speech.

"Hey, what a coincidence," my father said. "Ralph goes to college next week, and it's a school just down the road from Syracuse. Two great men heading north at once."

"Okay, I'll tell you what I'll do," said my Uncle Bill. "I'll fly him right up there with me."

"In the police plane?" said my father.

"That's the one."

"Bill, wonderful!"

"And then the troopers can take us right to the school."

I felt my stomach go into reverse. Arriving at college with state troopers would have been all right for the Shah of Iran or for an American under arrest, but such an entrance by me into a staid old school like Hamilton seemed a little less desirable than parachuting in. I made this point to my father, but he felt that the trip with O'Dwyer and the troopers would be going away to college first-class, a moment denied to him because he had failed to accept the challenge of the seventh grade.

"It'll be something you'll always remember, Poop," he said, using the nickname for me that, in a stunning lapse of imagination, I also used for him.

"But Hamilton's a classy little place," I said, "and I just can't go *into* it that way. I mean, *listen,* Poop, it's enough that I'm *Jewish.* Do I also need the *state police?*"

I was still debating these travel plans on the day that my father put my suitcase into a taxi for the ride to Gracie Mansion. We rode silently for a couple of minutes and then he suddenly took his face out of the *Daily News* and said, "Poop, you can smoke and drink now if you want, but be kind of careful with the women up there."

I was so embarrassed by his becoming Polonius that I was able to make no reply. I was also amused by the quaintness of this man, who had been smoking and drinking since he was ten, giving me his solemn permission to do so as a freshman of sixteen. I happened to have no desire to either smoke or drink, but I did sprout intermittent erections that I was never able to place and so a suggestion to be careful with women was hardly the coaching I needed right now.

This was the only traditional father-son talk we ever had; and it did not precisely qualify as that because, instead of speaking the role of the son, I merely chewed my fingernails. As we continued riding east, I waited for my father to talk more sex. He was both a boy of the streets and a man of Brooks Brothers and so I was hoping that he could tell me how to enter somebody's panties with an earthy yet elegant style; but the words "be kind of careful with women" were followed by no specific tips and they remained the only sexual data my father ever gave to me, except for when he said, "Al Capone died of syphilis, you know."

A few minutes later, as I rode to the airport in a Cadillac limousine, O'Dwyer turned to me and said, "Son, never forget the Constitution."

This seemed to be a political version of my father's sexual advice—what a day of momentous one-liners for me!—and again I awaited elaboration, though I didn't mind not receiving any because the Constitution concerned me less than my glands.

During the flight to Utica in a Police Department plane, I thought about my father's flair for extraordinary entrances. A month before, we had gone to a closed-circuit showing of a heavyweight championship fight at the Astor Theater in Times Square. The crowd outside the theater was dense and it didn't part like the Red Sea for us, but my father was always at his best in a crisis, especially one that threatened his prestige. He took out his press card and flashed it at a nearby sergeant of police, who was as impressed as if he had just been officially shown the jack of spades.

"Poop, what're we gonna *do?*" I said while somebody's elbow was exploring one of my kidneys. "I don't think we're gonna make it this time. We should've gotten *tickets.*"

Galvanized by hearing his son say such a defeatist word as "tickets," he suddenly crashed his way through the crowd and led me right up to the door.

"Everything all right here, captain?" he said to the officer in charge.

"All in good shape, sir," said the captain with a smart salute as my father and I walked into the theater to see Ezzard Charles defend his title as heavyweight champion of the world.

"Jesus, that's the greatest one you ever pulled," I told my father with the awe deserved by a man who had just impersonated a police inspector.

"Always do everything as if you belonged there," he replied.

And now I had to pretend that I belonged in a state police car that was taking a mayor and me to my school.

My God, I thought as the siren wailed, *I'll have to stay at Hamilton for postgraduate work to live this down.* I had, however, underrated my father's common sense, which sometimes broke through when he wasn't pretending to be an inspector of police. About a hundred yards from the dormitory in which I was to live, just as I was trying to climb into one of the car's ash trays, my father said, "Bill, let's get out here and walk the rest of the way."

O'Dwyer quickly stopped the car and the three of us walked up to the dorm; and when we reached it, O'Dwyer grabbed my heavy bag and took it inside, a gesture that delighted my father, who constantly waited for life to give him moments that could be pictures for page one.

That evening in the dorm, one of my roommates said to me, "I saw your old man carrying your bag when you came in."

"That wasn't my old man," I told him. "That was the Mayor of New York."

"And I'm the fuckin' Pope," he replied.

My father never knew the Pope, but he called Cardinal Spellman "Frank" at the annual "I Am an American Day," when the *Journal-American* lured thousands of immigrants to a glorious circulation boost at the Mall in Central Park. How my father enjoyed every moment of this event, from exchanging cordial lies with political hacks to persuading the cops to overestimate the crowd.

"Looks like a million here today, chief," my father would say while scanning eighty thousand immigrants, pickpockets, and bums.

"You could call it nearly a million, Paul," the police inspector would reply and my father would mentally write a headline that said JOURNAL OUTDRAWS ELLIS ISLAND.

One Sunday afternoon in June a year or two after the end of the war, this magical million in Central Park almost saw an incredible unrehearsed scene. A few minutes before the opening prayer, Irving Berlin told the publisher of the *Journal* that he would not share a stage with Kate Smith because he considered her a bigot who thought of Jews as "the little people." Of course, almost everybody, no matter what religion or race, was a little person compared to Kate Smith; but here was the composer of "God Bless America" refusing to sit beside the woman who had made the song a new national anthem.

At once the publisher came to my father and said, "Paul, we've got big trouble: Irving Berlin won't be seen with Kate Smith. He say she doesn't like Jews."

"Why don't we ask her?" said my father with a smile.

"Paul, he's *serious*. He may walk out."

"Relax, Joe, I'll handle him. Meanwhile, let's keep her away from him—we'll take her for pictures behind the bandstand—and we'd better warm up somebody else to sing the song—just in case. Maybe Bojangles could do it."

"That would be a lovely touch," the publisher said.

"Hey, wouldn't it be a helluva note," said my father, "if we found a picture of Kate Smith singing 'God Bless America' for the Klan?"

My father was unable to match his publisher's concern because the crisis was feeding his love of drama; and now he was savoring a headline that said BERLIN TO SMITH: "BLESS SOMETHING ELSE." And for the second edition, it could be freshened to say BERLIN TO SMITH: "KISS OFF, KATE."

Paul Schoenstein made Irving Berlin hold on to his seat on that Sunday in June, partly by persuasion "from one little person to another" and partly by singing to him the first few bars of "What'll I Do?" Only the thought of an embarrassment to his precious *Journal-American* had enabled my father to serenade America's greatest song writer without a drink.

On a Friday night a few months after that "I Am an American Day," I walked into the grand ballroom of Albany's DeWitt Clinton Hotel to meet my father at a dinner that was roasting Governor Dewey. The moment he saw me coming in, his arm shot up as if hailing a cab and he smiled glowingly and cried, "*Hey!*" Then he began introducing me to newspapermen with the words, "This is my son, Ralph, who's only great."

"Your father's told me a lot about you," seventeen people said to me.

There was, of course, nothing to tell except that I could hit a ball two sewers and had wet the bed until I was twelve; but nevertheless my father described me as if he were doing public relations for the baby Jesus. He had just given me a biography of Andrew Jackson that was inscribed *To the world's greatest man.*

"Are you going to win a Pulitzer Prize, too?" one of the reporters said to me.

"Oh . . . I don't know . . . I hope," I brightly said.

"It'll be the Nobel Prize for him," my father said.

He wasn't being merely proud or drunk, though he was sometimes both. He knew that the job I was dreaming of, Mister District Attorney, was never given a Pulitzer Prize. It was, however, fortunate that I changed dreams and became a writer instead of Manhattan's crusading D.A., for I would have had to put away a few of my father's friends, men like the judge at my bar mitzvah, who went on to celebrate services at the Allenwood Prison Farm.

The man being roasted at that Albany dinner had been a new Manhattan District Attorney in 1938 when my father, a new City Editor, had gotten some vital information for him about the underworld by having a reporter hold a racketeer's lover in a room at the Warwick Hotel for a week.

"Her name was Hope Dare," my father told me, "and she was gorgeous. I sent along a sob sister to get the stuff that Dewey needed and it was a historic moment for Hope: the first time she had ever been in a hotel room with a woman."

"The Warwick is a pretty swell place," I said.

"Of course. I always kidnap first-class."

It was ironic that my father's hobby was holding people in hotel rooms because he himself had claustrophobia and must have told me "No, no, don't close the door" even more often than he asked me "Who's the greatest man in the world?" I was always slow to reply to this question because it was one with two right answers, neither of which was Albert Schweitzer. The greatest man in the world was either one of us: we shared the title the way we shared his socks and ties and the name of Poop.

My father was careful about the other men to whom he put the question of who was the greatest man in the world, because some, like Dewey, would have named themselves; and so, on the night of the Albany dinner, my father and Dewey avoided analysis of their international splendor and instead sang "The Sidewalks of New York" as a duet for two baritones. I looked at my father with his arm around Dewey, a man as embraceable as a statue, and I wondered if any other boy was lucky enough to have a father who got more intimate with the Governor than Mrs. Dewey did.

Dewey was my father's best chance to move up from Mister New York to Mister United States; but Dewey fell short of the White House because of a personal quirk— total insensitivity—that I saw displayed on a night in the forties when he gave my father and me a lift after seeing a fight at the Polo Grounds. As our car with the license NY 1 and the police escort moved into Harlem, Dewey told the driver to turn the siren on for me. When it began to sound, I stupidly began to wave at the surly black faces on the garbage-filled streets; and more than one of them must have mused, *Who is the little white motherfucker that needs an air-raid drill to get home?*

My father, however, was not upset that Dewey was waking half of Harlem as a little entertainment for me.

Paul Schoenstein was once again traveling first-class, this time returning triumphantly to the unlikely neighborhood where his family had lived as a little lost tribe of Israel.

"I was born right over there—off Lenox Avenue—and it was a dull day when I didn't have at least a couple of fights," he said as the siren screamed and Dewey grinned and I waved like a pygmy king at the people who were deciding to vote for Harry Truman. "Sometimes you would say good morning to a guy before you hit him in the mouth and sometimes you would skip the etiquette."

"But what was your family doing up *here?*" I said. "I mean, you were *white.*"

"Oh, yeah, we were always white," he replied, "but it was all we could afford. My father was a bookbinder and he would've done okay if anyone in Harlem had known how to read. He should've been a book*maker* like everybody else."

Many years after our conquest of Harlem, when I was doing a column for the *Journal-American,* my father had another chance to attach himself to a rising Republican: I brought to his office a handsome young Congressman named John V. Lindsay, whom I had called a "Republican Kennedy." As Lindsay and I approached the city desk, my father's hand shot up and he cried, "Hey, Mister President!"

I cringed and felt enraged, for I had asked my father not to treat Lindsay as if he were the poster boy for the March of Dimes. However, to be taken seriously by my father, you had to be either the Governor, the Mayor, or my mother.

"Nice to see you, Mister President," he said while I smilingly ground my teeth and fixed him with a look that said, *For God's sake, Poop, he's a* Congressman, *so cut the patronizing crap!*

But Lindsay, like Dewey, was a man with an Episcopalian smile and my father preferred the politicians who were lit from within. The night that this light left Jimmy Walker, my father conquered his dread of hospitals to be one of two people who sat with Walker at Doctors Hospital till he died. And on the morning of the funeral, my father played a splendidly offbeat role for a Jewish boy: he was the doorman of St. Patrick's Cathedral, where he stood on the steps and told the police which people could be let inside. Had Rabbi Neumann seen him smartly directing all that Catholic traffic, he would have said in pious disgust, "Well, what can you expect from the man who gives his son a Ringling Brothers bar mitzvah?"

For almost an hour, my father commanded those steps as if he were a maître d' and St. Patrick's were a theological Toots Shor's. A few minutes before the mass began, a beefy man he had turned away was heard to angrily ask a cop, "Who does that bastard think he is?"

I could have told him the answer, of course. The bastard thought he was Mister New York.

3

FAREWELL, MISTER FIXIT

Late one afternoon in spring when I was about eleven years old, I was playing touch football in Riverside Park, romping over condoms that had been left on the lawn by sailors who'd been trying just as hard to score in other sports on the previous night. I was dashing madly about to get free for a pass from Freddie Cohen, who was my hero, not only because he could throw a football a sewer-and-a-half but also because he knew how to masturbate in the children's section of Loew's 83rd. This combination of Freddie's passing arm and pelvic bravado had turned me into his slave. On the football field, I ran amok to catch the passes he threw; and while Van Johnson was taking off to bomb Tokyo on the silver screen, I made sure that the only erection the matron could see was the American flag.

On this particular spring afternoon, I had just smothered a pass from Freddie in the place where my chest should have been when a policeman appeared and gave us a summons for playing football on the grass, which New York's Sun King, Robert Moses, had planted to grow untrod by man in those bucolic days of World War II. Even the great Freddie was rendered helpless by this summons and could only say, "What the fuck is this?", an inquiry he had often been heard to make about biology at school.

And then an incredible bit of timing took place: a taxicab suddenly stopped at the field and out came my other boyhood hero, Superpop. He quickly crossed the lawn to us and said, "What's going on here?"

"He gave us a ticket for playing ball," I said, holding the summons in the air.

My father looked at it for a moment and then his temper exploded, a temper that had frightened me since the first time I saw him try to reshape my sister's behind with a bedroom slipper. Clenching his teeth, he snatched the summons from my hand, tore it up, and said to the cop, "For Crissake, why don't you go after Luciano and leave a bunch of kids alone!"

The cop was so flabbergasted by my father's quick reduction of that ticket that he mumbled something to try to save face and then walked away to look for enemies more conventional than the Lone Ranger of Riverside Park.

That moment of gridiron drama set a pattern of applying the fix to my life that my father was to follow for many years. Making a fix, in fact, was such a fundamental part of his style, such a matter of pride and delight to him, that he seemed incapable of doing anything the ordinary way.

"I'd love to see that eclipse tonight," I once told him.

"I'll call George Solitaire and get you a couple of tickets," he said.

I was, of course, hardly the only one favored by this Jewish godfather of mine. He fixed traffic tickets for Hearstmen who were busy with crusades about civic duty; he got people into hospitals, out of jails, and around customs men; he fixed a disorderly-conduct charge against one of the sons of William Randolph Hearst who had spent his life being Citizen Drunk; and he even was part of what must have been America's first fixed radio show: he refused to be a guest detective on "Ellery Queen" unless the producer first told him the killer, a name he forgot by the middle commercial because, when not editing his paper, he had the attention span of a flea.

Of all his fixes, however, only those that he pulled off for his son were followed by a little speech. Every time he made things too easy for me by taking me to the front of a line or having a reporter drive me home from school or getting the Army to station me in the lobby of the Astor Hotel, he would say, "My father was never able to do this for me." During my father's own boyhood days in the Harlem of pre-World War I, Rudolph Schoenstein had done so badly as a bookbinder that his youngest child, Paul, one of six children, had been forced to wear his brother's old shoes; and so my father went on to become a man who bought shoes the way other people buy socks.

Because of his daring style, because he was City Editor of the biggest evening paper in America, and because he had arms like a well-manicured ape, my father seemed to me a giant when I was growing up. During the 1940s, every boy was supposed to think that his own father was Superman, but mine just happened to be: not a mild-mannered reporter who put on a cape in a telephone booth, but a commanding editor who could use a telephone booth to get tickets to any sold-out Broadway show. He had so much strength in just his hands that I liked to have him take Freddie's wrist between his two fingers and then squeeze it, smiling that boyish smile of his as if he were merely taking a pulse, until Freddie cried, "*Jesus*, Mr. S., *okay!*" Like a pint-sized fight promoter, I was constantly looking for people who wanted to trade punches with my father, a search that should have been easy, for there were thousands of liberals in my neighborhood to whom punching an editor with Hearst would have seemed like a moment on New Year's Eve.

"Hey, you wanna go shot-for-shot with my old man?" I asked a brawny boy in school one day.

"What is he, a bouncer or somethin'?" the boy replied.

"No, he edits," I said. "Shot-for-shot is just on the side. If you want, he'll do the arm you don't write with."

In my entire boyhood, I heard few lines as intoxicating as the one I heard when Freddie solemnly said to me, "Ralphie, whaddaya think would happen if your father ever hit anybody with all his might?"

"He'd kill the bastard!" I said in an orgasm of pride. "My father was a longshoreman, you know."

That was a lie: he had been a seaman; but every time I

embroidered the truth, I was using my father's favorite stitch.

"A *longshoreman?*" said Freddie. "No kiddin'."

"Goddam right. A longshoreman's fists are like a fighter's, you know: they're deadly weapons."

"And they gotta be registered with the police?"

"My father could register, sure. He's just too busy catching spies for the paper."

My father's strength, achievements, and connections simply stated were impressive enough; but I had inherited his flair for hyperbole, his Hearstian touch, and so whenever I talked about him, I shoveled the shit like a circus hand.

Although he never came close to killing anybody, my father had the kind of temper that would have made him an excellent Hun. Whenever this temper erupted, whenever he tightened his jaw and slammed a door or a table or the receiver of a phone, I found myself terrified. Eventually I developed a supersensitivity to rage; and because of it, I have never been able to enjoy a good fight with my wife.

There was no doubt that my father could have licked every other father on the block, but a middleweight nun could have done the same, so I promoted no matches with these men. One of them was a skinny asthmatic, one wore glasses that looked like blocks of ice, and all the rest seemed elderly, while my father always seemed about thirty-five. I can still see him coming home from the *Journal-American* in the days when he lived *The Front*

Page: his thick dark hair brushed straight back, his stride still jaunty after nine hours in the city room, his arms holding the last editions of New York's four evening newspapers and maybe a book or a game for me; or maybe boxing gloves that had been worn by Henry Armstrong or the actual script of the Fred Allen Show; or maybe the galleys of one of my stories that he had proudly had set in his composing room, the only composing room in America where a ten-year-old's salutes to Sid Luckman and Mel Ott were put into type during breaks in attacks on Eleanor Roosevelt. I can still see him stepping from a cab as I put my head out of a sixth-story window to drop a water bomb on a woman below, whom my puckishly patriotic mind saw as a Japanese battleship with a peroxide deck. My father, however, is playing a real war game, for he has stopped to say good night to those two F.B.I. agents who have been following him to learn how he has uncovered German espionage.

"I have to be nice to them," he told me with a smile one night. "They're both *Journal* readers."

My father's one-upmanship with the Feds gave me a status on the block as great as if I'd been seduced by my mother's maid. One of my friends, a boy with a partial IQ named Max, said that his father knew The Shadow; but to blithely patronize two federal agents in front of your house was tangible and awesome glamour indeed.

Moreover, I learned from my father that the F.B.I. had also been tapping our phone, a piece of news so incredible that it made me call Maurey and say, "Hello, Number

One, this is Number Two. The material left Hong Kong at 2400 hours. It's hidden in the false bottom of a Trojan. Your rendezvous will be somewhere in the 72nd Street toilet of the uptown IRT."

"Who the hell is this—Ralphie?" Maurey said.

"Ralphie is up the cow's ass," I replied, gleefully picturing an F.B.I. agent who wished he had studied dentistry instead. "Here are your instructions, Number One. Set your decoder. First word . . . Fox . . . Uncle . . . Charlie . . . King . . . Second word . . . Tear . . . Hero . . . Easy . . . Third word . . . Fox . . . Baker . . . Item."

"Hey, Ralphie, you losin' your *mind?*" said Maurey, playing dumb convincingly. I was grateful for his help in making the smoke screen that was providing protection for Paul Schoenstein, Counterspy.

I must have been insufferable during my boyhood because I spent it father-dropping: either bragging about something he had done, such as inventing penicillin, or presenting him in person to friends, as if I were master of ceremonies of a show called "Can You Top Pop?" In the late forties, I went to Stuyvesant High School, which was full of budding scientists and fully flowered socialists. The scientists had their heads in their tubes, but the socialists were the most politically conscious punks around and they dressed me again in the scarlet H that I had worn in grammar school. This time, however, I turned my father loose on them by bringing him to school one day to address the Journalism Club.

"Do you have any dirt on Norman Thomas?" I said as I led him toward a room where he would be greeted as if he wanted to repeal the child-labor laws.

"I can handle myself with these wise guys," he said; and moments later, I saw that he could.

"Why does the *Journal-American* use those awful red headlines?" said a boy who had some mustard on his chin.

"Do you think they're Communistic?" my father said and some of the Marx brothers laughed.

"They're undignified," the boy replied.

"So is the news. And by the way, they're not always red. On St. Patrick's Day, they're green."

There was more laughter in the room. The boy was learning what I already knew: that my father had a talent for charming non sequitur that sabotaged rational debate.

"Why does the *Journal-American* print Pegler and Sokolsky and all those other reactionaries?" another boy said.

"Why does this school have all types of students?" my father replied, taking note of Stuyvesant's melting pot of socialists, Socialist Workers, and Socialist Laborites.

"But the *Journal-American* has reactionaries and nobody *else.*"

"It has me and I voted for Roosevelt," my father said. "But please don't tell Mr. Hearst."

The boys laughed again and their hostility seemed to be draining away. Karl Marx hadn't told them that humor is also an opiate of the masses.

"Why can't the *Journal-American* be more like the

Times?" said a boy whose fly was open, a popular fashion at Stuyvesant.

"And why can't you be more like Einstein?" said my father in his Brooks Brothers suit.

"Your analogy is invalid. Einstein isn't a student here, but you and the *Times* are both newspapers."

I could sense that my father was afraid to deliver what might be another insult to the boy, so he detoured into his commercial:

"Are you aware, my friend, that the *Journal-American* tells you ten times as much about New York as the *Times?* —unless you want the cribbage scores. And we *care* about the city, too; we have a heart—in fact, half the calls I get are from people asking for help. We've gotten pets for poor children at Christmas and we've found kids who've run away and we just built a home for those quadruplets in the Bronx and we're getting the veterans to turn in their guns and we also just proved that most of the divorces in this state are phony."

"How'd you do that?" said the boy.

"A woman named Sarah Ellis came to me and said that she was part of a ring that faked evidence of adultery for divorces. I kept her in a hotel room for a week until we could check out the cases she named."

"You kept her in a *hotel* room?" said the boy and a few of his friends laughed salaciously.

"My, what lively ideas you have," said my father with a smile.

At last there was rapport between the Hearstman and

the sons of Debs, for these boys were even more devoted to getting laid than to social reform. Every one of them would have gladly gone to bed with Eva Perón.

After the meeting of the club had ended, I walked with my father to the *Journal-American* radio car that was waiting outside the school.

"Did your old man do all right with the Commies today?" he said. He often needed such reassurance, for he was an insecure Superman.

"You were terrific, Poop," I replied.

"I like you to be proud of me. Someday you'll be able to tell them that your father was okay."

"I tell them right now," I said uneasily. I was always embassassed by sentiment from my father, whose talk often called for a gypsy violin.

"That kid thought I didn't know the meaning of invalid analogy," he said. "The little bubblehead."

"He didn't know your vocabulary, Poop," I said to the man who never failed to define any word I brought to him. "You should have called him a feckless fellow."

"No, a fustian shit." And the two of us laughed. "You need any money?" he said.

This was the way we always parted: not with "Goodbye" but "You need any money?" It was a style that he passed on to me, for every morning when my daughters leave for school I find myself seeding them with coins; and they are seeds that are watered at night when the girls' jingling jeans reach the washing machine and I think of my father's favorite line about the rich: "His hobby is washing his money."

And so back and forth I swung in the shadow of Paul Schoenstein: from having things made hard for me because he worked for Hearst to having things made easy for me by his financing and his love of the fix. All his fixing, however, turned out to be merely practice for the greatest challenge of his life, the one that put him in a class with Mussolini, Pancho Villa, and Roy Cohn: trying to defeat the Army of the United States.

The day my father took me to the Army Induction Center began like most other days in a life that had nothing but his family and his work: the city desk called him at six o'clock and he coughed himself awake and lit a cigarette, once again daring his lungs to find air. After talking to the desk about the coverage for the day, he made four glasses of orange juice, a cup of coffee for himself, and a glass of chocolate milk for me. Looking back on those breakfasts, I feel a nostalgic nausea, for the blend of tepid orange juice and cold chocolate milk was my father's loving emetic for me. I see now that those meals needed something and this something I suspect was food.

On that rainy morning in early October of 1953, after drinking our breakfast, my father and I went down to the street, where he hailed a cab by whistling with his two index fingers in his mouth. If my father had not been an editor, he could have made a fine doorman, for his whistle could be heard a block away, he had the strength to lift any bags, and he could always remember where he had hidden a bottle of gin. By the time I was drafted, my father was giving me the honor of being his underground bartender in a private version of Prohibition, with my mother playing a Fed. The moment the two of us were alone, he ordered silently by using two fingers to indicate a needed shot; and then I would sneak him one that sat much better than his chocolate milk sat with me.

As we rode together toward my new life, with my father going through the *Daily Mirror* and *Daily News,* I kept anticipating his speech, wondering if he was going to warn me to be careful of clap and hand grenades; but he surprised me by sending me off to the wars with just a tender little promise that he would be my Commander-in-Chief.

"I don't want you to worry, because I'm going to take care of everything," he said. "Just do what they tell you for the time being."

My father was arranging my defense of the country the way he arranged my bar-mitzvah day. True to a cherished American tradition, he believed that the military should be under civilian control.

When our cab arrived at the Induction Center, he kissed me wetly on the cheek and I forced myself not to pull away. My daughters accuse me of giving wet kisses, but my lips are merely moist. My father, however, could irrigate a face, not only a woman's but also a man's.

"Call me when you get to Fort Dix," he said. "And don't forget to show them your feet."

The feet he had in mind were the ones whose genes for flatness had come from him; and the doctor at my pre-induction physical was clearly impressed when I proudly said, "Did you ever see feet as flat as these?"

"Certainly not," he said. "You may have some trouble marching on them. Next man."

My father would have sent a reporter to bring me a pair of roller skates, but he had already made his doctor give me a letter that said I was able to stand for no more than twenty minutes at a time. I carried this letter uneasily, for it did not seem precisely consistent with the business of leaving home and becoming a man; and it also could have given the Army a chance to let me pull guard duty on my knees.

As the bus took me and the other recruits down the New Jersey Turnpike toward Fort Dix, I began to wonder if my induction would make the Russians consider reopening the Korean War. With my scrawny body, my myopic eyes, and my doctor's suggestion that I be allowed to soldier from a golfing cart, I was a one-man demilitarization for an Army that could have drafted nothing drearier. I didn't know that a few seats behind me was equivalent dreariness: a man named G. David Schine, a millionaire flunky for Senator Joseph McCarthy, whose dilettantish duty at Dix would cause the Congressional investigation that brought McCarthy to his end.

After flaunting my feet had done no good, I knew I was out of defective parts and so I surrendered myself to eight weeks of basic training for the infantry, with my father phoning supplementary and contradictory commands:

"Be tough, Poop . . . Don't worry, I'm taking care of things . . . Be a man . . . That colonel knows who your father is . . . This is a very good test for you . . . Would it help you to have a press card?"

At the beginning of December, I was struck by coughing, wheezing, chills, and a fever of 102. Since 103 was needed for admission to the Fort Dix hospital, all I could do was enrich my medical file with a note from a doctor that said: *This man has pneumonia. Light duty for 24 hours.*

"You got any penicillin left at the *Journal?*" I asked my father that night after poignantly describing my bronchial tubes.

"I hope you're not letting them push you around," he said.

"They're *supposed* to push me around," I told him.

"Then why aren't you in the hospital?"

"I didn't score high enough with a thermometer to qualify for being sick."

My father's duty now was clear: to have me moved to an Army post where the hospital wasn't run like a rifle range. Three weeks later, when my training was done, a general who owed him a favor had me transferred to the Public Information Office of First Army Headquarters at Governors Island, New York, the kind of assignment that would have followed the drafting of Faust. Not only was it a setting for a college musical, this sleepy little campus off Manhattan's southern tip, but I didn't even have to sleep there: I was allowed to live at home and commute each day to national defense. I was somewhere between a sunshine soldier and a soldier named G. David Schine, who now was making sure that the Stork Club remained a part of the Non-Communist World.

No member of my family had ever served in the military and I was carrying on this tradition by having reveille with John Gambling, then combat in the IRT, and then a landing on an island to write releases that saluted the toughness of the First Army man. Some days, however, I got up later for special flack missions to midtown magazines. My soldiering was so offbeat that one morning my mother said to me, "Ralph, do you have Army today?"

Press-agentry duty on Governors Island was shameful enough, but worse shame lay ahead for me because my father liked to keep topping himself.

"It's a nuisance to have to keep taking that ferry twice a day, isn't it?" he said to me as he mopped up some stew with Italian bread at dinner one night.

"Oh no, I *love* the ferry," I said, afraid of what he had in mind. "It gives me a feeling of serving overseas."

"Well, I was talking to Harry at Toots' last night and he said you could help with the PIO at the Armed Forces Committee."

"Where's that?" I said, wanting no reply.

"Three forty-six Broadway." He smiled. "There's a unit at the Astor Hotel, but there are no openings right now."

"Poop, the Schine thing is a *national scandal*," I said. "And when they finish with him, we're next. You'll make McCarthy look like a *patriot*."

In spite of this speech, my father insisted on continuing his war games and I found myself transferred to the Manhattan mainland, where I took an elevator to my post and my mess hall was called Chock Full o'Nuts.

I had been marching through Broadway for less than a month when orders suddenly came for me to report to Fort Lewis, Washington, the port of embarkation for the Far East Command. The rumor I heard during coffee breaks was that someone at First Army Headquarters didn't like the way I was heading toward a bivouac at the Essex House.

"Please don't mess with these orders, Poop," I said. "I think I'd *like* to go overseas."

"Well, do you mind if I get you assigned to Clark Field in Honolulu?" he asked. "You may even have a few half-brothers there." He often joked about distributing his genes in Honolulu after having jumped from a Luckenbach ship.

I was still weak enough to be tempted by a post on Honolulu instead of demanding a chance to be sent to Korea, Okinawa, or Japan; and so I went to Fort Lewis with visions of a voyage to Clark Field. They were visions like the ones of Columbus for traveling west to reach Cathay: I learned from a bellboy in Seattle that Clark Field was in the Philippines. Such were my father's powers, however, that I felt he still might have had it moved.

"Poop," I said on the phone from Fort Lewis, "Clark Field is in the Philippines."

"Jesus, when did that happen?" he said.

"I think that it's always been there."

"Okay, we'll make it Pearl Harbor then."

"No, that's a naval base and I'm in the Army. At least I *think* I am."

The following day, this Army, unaware that I was a freelance soldier, gave me orders to go to Japan and be a press agent for the Far East Command. Now it was my father's turn to order in this embarrassing game of Simon Says; but his final move merely caused me to be called before a major, who said in an icy Southern voice, "Son, is somebody pullin' strings for you?"

"Why—no, sir," I said, pretending I didn't know a puppeteer named Poop.

"Well, your goddam Congressman has asked us to hold you here 'cause he thinks that you're needed in America. Now, son, does America really need *you*?"

"No, sir, I'm sure it doesn't."

"And will your Mommy and Daddy cry if we send your ass all the way to Japan?"

"Sir, my ass is all yours," I said.

"Who the hell is your daddy, anyway?"

I should have put my father at that whorehouse piano, but instead I said, "He's the City Editor of the *Journal-American*."

"All you Jewish gentlemen are writers, aren't you?" the major said.

I was stunned for a moment and then I said, "Oh no—
we have Hank Greenberg, Justice Frankfurter, and Dinah
Shore."

When I left that major, I felt smaller than I'd felt at any
time since leaving the womb; and I was angry at his bigo-
try and at my father's coddling of me and at myself for
forgetting to mention that Mel Allen was Jewish, too.

"He spoke to *you* that way?" said my father on the
telephone that night and I could see his cheek muscles
tighten and his teeth begin to grind. "The Christian Front-
ing son of a bitch! The lousy little pants presser!"

Rage had caused my father to mix his epithets, for although most pants pressers have been Jewish, whenever
he wanted to describe somebody as a lesser being, my
father called him a pants presser. And a pants presser the
major surely was, with a crease that could have cut liver-
wurst.

"I'll take care of that bastard!" my father said.

"Poop, I really wish you—I mean, what the hell are you
gonna do?"

Since he had failed to help me by taking my case to
Congress and Toots Shor's, I was afraid that his next move
might be a call to the Hearst candidate for President,
Douglas MacArthur, who knew the difference between
Japan and Clark Field because he had worked as God at
both.

Seven days later, I carried my twenty-minute standing
slip and my *Journal-American* press card up the gang-
plank of the U.S.S. *Mitchell* and there was still no pro-

nouncement from MacArthur saying, "He shall return." I boarded that ship as a twenty-one-year-old baby who wanted my orthopedic shoes to be back on the floor of the Astor Roof, to be letting Sally Schneiderman's splendidly convex chest fill the concavity of my own as I dreamily shoved her around to "Sunday, Monday, or Always." I was plaintively sailing in the direction that my father had sailed when he was twenty-one but twice my age. He often had told me of his fistfights with other seamen on the Luckenbach Line, but I was a pugilistic virgin and just once removed from the other kind, too. In the summer of 1952, I had made a brief deposit with a prostitute in Paris who could have been mistaken for a still life.

On the six-day voyage to Japan, I lost myself in *The Caine Mutiny,* the story of a spoiled boy who was forced to become a man at sea; and mentally I felt that now was the moment for me to cut the cord that tied me to the *Journal* city room; but emotionally I still wanted my father to pick up the phone and tell the captain to give me a better table. Day after day, I dumped garbage into the ocean while my spirits sank to the bottom as well.

When I reached Japan, the cord was stretching seven thousand miles. My father called me once a week, daring the Japanese operators to say Schoenstein, which would have been a better wartime password for American troops than "lalapalooza."

"I can do anything with a phone," my father liked to tell the world; and one such feat was to call Japan with absolutely nothing to say.

"How's everything, Poop?" he would half shout.

"Fine, Poop, just fine," I would reply, deciding that this was not the time to mention my only piece of news: the nonspecific urethritis that I had picked up from a person or persons unknown in Tokyo. This VD for the beginner might have made my father proud; but saying "nonspecific urethritis" on that uncertain overseas line also might have made him think that I had terrific tonsillitis and he would have flown a surgeon to me.

"Is everything okay with you?" he would say again, not having listened to my first report.

"Absolutely. I'm seeing lots of temples and shrines and —how is everybody there?"

"Do you need any money?"

The most memorable call of my Japanese days was the one he arranged for me to make through a loudspeaker in Lüchow's restaurant to greet the guests at a celebration of his twenty-fifth anniversary. Because of the import of this connection, I wrote a two-page speech that was full of references to relatives who would be coming into heat at the sound of my disembodied voice. Moreover, my script began with a couple of lines of Japanese that were written for me by a gracious bilingual bimbo who had charged no extra for editorial services. I had forgotten, however, to consider my father's attention span for talk, even when he was paying exorbitant rates to have it piped in; and so when I picked up the phone at Camp Zama and began to speak in Japanese, my father took five words and then cried, "God bless you, Ralph! We love you too!"

In spite of the source of my Japanese, it contained no reference to love. I quickly returned to being cutely inscrutable, but my father could take only two more words and may even have started to wonder if the voice in the speaker had called the wrong anniversary.

"Say hello to your mother!" he cried. "In English!"

I had put a few lines about my mother in the speech and now I stopped to search for them while the international air went dead. I was in the unique position of being unable to ad-lib a hello to my mother on her anniversary day. Things sometimes went like that when my father and I were both involved.

In addition to his regular weekly calls, a letter came from him almost every day, five or six lines quickly done in pencil at his desk so I could have such bulletins as *Good morning, Poop!* and *Are your geishas holding out?* and *How's the greatest soldier in Japan?* The greatest soldier in Japan was fine because Maxwell Taylor took care of himself; but I probably had a few more dollars in my pocket than he did, because his father didn't send him cash. All of it came by mail, with one enchanting exception: an attractive female reporter with an assignment in Tokyo brought me one hundred new dollar bills, the first time any girl in Tokyo had ever given money to *me*.

While my father was writing notes that should have been sold as greeting cards, I was writing a book about a military career somewhere between those of Beetle Bailey and Benedict Arnold. One morning I was standing at the International News Service wire machine in the Public

Information Office of the Far East Command, looking for plugs for my Army, when the most powerful columnist in Hollywood, Louella Parsons, suddenly said:

Ralph Schoenstein, son of the *Journal-American*'s Pulitzer Prize-winning City Editor Paul, is a corporal in Japan whose book exposing the Army, *But I Always Called Them Sir*, will be published soon.

I tried not to panic but I failed, for my position now was like that of a man who had just been caught writing *Hitler sucks* on a Berchtesgaden wall. It was less than ten minutes until the colonel in charge of the office was saying to me with quiet disgust, "Corporal, are you aware of the regulation that personnel on active duty cannot write books about the Army?"

"Yes, sir," I said above the slamming of my heart.

"Do you know what's happening to Colonel Voorhees for keeping that diary about Korea?"

"Yes, sir, I do."

"And if we're doing that to a full colonel, what do you think we could do to *you?*"

I desperately explained that the transmissions of Louella Parsons were as reliable as those of Tokyo Rose; but for a man raised by military gospel and not the hearsay of Hearst, anything on a wire machine was uncontestable.

"I want to see this book," he said.

"Sir, there *is* no book," I told him. "And it hasn't been accepted anyway—I mean, my *notes* for it haven't . . . I mean . . ."

"Corporal, on my desk tomorrow will either be a copy of your book or the original of your court-martial papers."

Moments later, I called my father and said that my return to the States might be delayed because I had to serve a prison term first.

"Poop, did *you* tell that jackass Parsons the book had been accepted?" I said.

"Of course not," he replied, lying as smoothly as he always had. "*You* know that Lollipops can barely spell."

"Well, you can help her spell court-martial. I broke a big regulation—at least they *think* I did—and the colonel is ready to eat me alive!"

"Now just relax and stop worrying. I'll call him and straighten the whole thing out."

"Dammit, you've gotta stop straightening everything *out* for me!" I cried, in a rare display of anger at him.

"Okay," he said with an edge. "I *won't* straighten it out."

I was silent for a couple of seconds and then I said, "Well, just one more," and both of us laughed.

He not only convinced the colonel that a book by me did not exist: he dispensed so much charm that the colonel was almost convinced that Louella Parsons did not exist. And then my father offered him a job on the *Journal-American* when he was done with active duty. It was Mr. Fixit's finest hour, this capture of the enemy.

A few weeks later, the Army sent me to Dacca, East Pakistan, a wretchedly hot and filthy spot, whose claim to be called Asshole of the World could have been challenged only by French Guiana and by Utica, New York.

In what seemed like atonement for writing my book, I was now to write about some medics who had gone to battle cholera in the flood plain of East Pakistan; and I welcomed the hardship of this trip because I need a little suffering in a place that my father couldn't call.

Early one evening soon after my arrival, I was standing in the muddy courtyard of a barracks outside Dacca, entertaining some Pakistani soldiers with squirts of a Burma-Shave lather bomb. Had they known that their amusement was coming from a Jewish infidel, they might have turned to even richer diversion and removed my testicles. The captain had warned us to be careful of our behavior with our Moslem hosts, for they seemed to spend a lot of time just waiting around to take offense. We were never to walk on the big flat stone in the courtyard that was used for prayer and we were never to touch or even look hard at any of the local women, who in 1954 wore purdah veils.

"Gentlemen," the captain had said, "to photograph these women is just as bad as fucking them"; and so I risked neither exposure and limited my ejaculations to shaving cream.

My lather show was about to end when a sergeant came running to me with a piece of paper on which were written three words: TELEPHON CORPOREL SHIENNTIN

Since there were no Chinese troops in the area, I knew that the phone call was for me. As I followed the sergeant through soggy grass to a small house that had an ancient phone, I suddenly thought, *The crazy bastard has got the record!* My father was making the longest long-distance call that could be made, for Pakistan was precisely half-way around the world from New York. Moreover, the achievement would be doubly memorable because he un-doubtedly was making the call to give me the score of the Giants game.

I shouted my name into the phone, heard a few seconds of static, and then the familiar cry of the lone arranger came to me:

"Hello, *Poop?*"

"*Jesus,* Poop," I shouted, "I don't *believe* it! You've made *history!*"

It wasn't mainstream history, of course, but he *had* suc-ceeded in connecting a Hearst city room with a Bengal swamp.

"Have you seen the Taj Mahal?"

"It's not in Pakistan," I said. "It's at Clark Field."

He didn't laugh because, as usual, he was listening only to his end.

"God bless you, Poop!" he cried, feeling that the dis-tance we had bridged called for more than just the Giants' score. "Do you need any money?"

"No, thanks, there's nothing to spend it on."

"I've told Winchell you're working with the medics down there."

"Jesus, you're *impossible!* Just make sure he doesn't have me in command of India." I could see the Winchell item already:

It's curtains for leprosy in Asia now that Major Ralph Schoenstein, the fighting son of "Penicillin Paul," has gone to war
against bad skin.

"Watch out for snakes with dysentery," said my father
in a line I perhaps misheard, for his voice now was fading
in and out.

When our conversation was over, I began to laugh out
loud; and as I jogged back into the courtyard, my mind
was still giddy with telephonic triumph while my feet
were crossing the holy stone. There was sudden agitation
among the Pakistanis and in my lower intestine as well, for
I was struck by the horror of what I had done. I felt like
shouting, *Allah would want you to forgive the lather man!*
I knew that they were asking themselves, *What would
Allah want done with the defiler in the orthopedic shoes?*

Moments later, I faced my captain and he was nothing if
not direct:

"Schoenstein, you dumb son of a bitch, didn't I *tell* you
to keep your goddam feet away from that fucking holy
stone? Didn't I *tell* you how careful we have to be to
respect the customs of these greaseballs? Well, they either
want a big fat apology from you or maybe they just want
you. They can have you, of course."

Awaiting my fate, I felt a strange intoxication from my
newest mess. That ancient phone could surely never reach
the city room again; moreover I didn't want it to. The time
had finally come for me to fix one by myself. Maybe I
could get out of it merely by renouncing my bar mitzvah;

or maybe I would have to sweep out a few mosques; but no matter what happened to me, it was suddenly wonderful to know that I was beyond the help of Paul Schoenstein or his friend the Aga Khan.

4

AREN'T YOU PAUL'S SON?

On Labor Day evening of 1955, I sat with my father on the terrace of our East End Avenue apartment and looked southward at my dream: a giant neon sign in midtown that said RCA, calling me to conquer the communications world of New York. To the east, across the river in Queens, a sign that said PEARL-WICK HAMPERS offered an alternate and more reachable dream; but the son of the greatest City Editor in America had to aim higher than a company that helped to package dirty clothes.

"Always remember that your name is Schoenstein," my father used to say.

He was speaking to one of the very few people who *could* remember it, for I was often called Schoenfeld, Shorenstein, Shanestein, and others nearby in the telephone book; and therefore I felt a challenge to carry high the family name, the lifting of which had produced so many linguistic hernias.

This challenge was enriched by another problem that I faced on that warm September night: even in obscurity, my own identity still didn't exist: my father's friends wouldn't stop calling me Paul.

"I'm Ralph," I would say on the phone to some Hearst-man who was giving my father the privilege of getting him into a Broadway show or out of an Off-Broadway traffic court.

Even my father didn't call me Ralph: his name for me was always Poop, the nickname I had given to *him* to tease him about getting tired too early in the tennis games we sometimes played; but I forgave his plagiarism because he was an editor and never a writer. The story in *Coronet* that ran under his byline, *I Am a City Editor*, was written by me when I was nineteen for a magazine editor who said to me, "Paul, I'm glad to see you're on your way to being a writer like your dad." Had I been pointed toward such a goal, I would have been writing lists of stories for reporters to cover and notes to my mother to clean my ties. The only memorable writing that my father ever did was to inscribe the new books that he gave me with such lines as *To a future Hemingway,* an inscription that comes to mind whenever I'm inclined to shoot myself. He liked the sound of this inscription so much that during my boyhood he used the same style on the flyleaves of several other books. By the time I was twelve, he had told me I would be a future Oliver Wendell Holmes, a future Robert Benchley, and a future Phil Riz-zuto; and so there was pressure on me to become a Su-preme Court judge who made one-reelers and could go to his left.

Because my father's literary talent was limited to such

prophecies, the breathless tabloid prose of *I Am a City Editor* was entirely mine, lines that undoubtedly speeded the disappearance of *Coronet:*

I am a City Editor. And the legends about my glamorous life—surrounded by sin, mystery, and romance—well, they just aren't true.

Being a City Editor means many things. It means I am manager, director, and midwife of at least five editions daily—editions changing with lightning-like speed to keep up with the swift march of events. It means that when a plane crashes just after midnight, I will be awakened, then when Arnold Schuster, who fingered the notorious Willie Sutton, is shot at nine in the evening, I will be pulled out of a barber chair.

I work—and work hard—ten hours a day in a bustling City Room on the sixth floor of a huge building overlooking the East River in lower New York. It's a day that starts at 6 a.m., when the telephone awakens me, a day that ends whenever the phone is merciful enough to stop ringing. It is no novelty for me to be awakened at midnight by one of my 64 reporters. Shall he take the next plane to Los Angeles to follow a murder clue? Shall he give up his vigil outside the home of a racketeer?

Like the proverbial housewife, my day is never done.

Meanwhile, back on the terrace at the end of that Labor Day, Hearst's proverbial housewife was blithely writing down all the people who didn't know that my name was Ralph and were going to launch me on a career of writing as well as Paul Schoenstein. It wasn't easy for us to decide if we should let Walter Winchell, Dorothy Kilgallen, Ed Sullivan, Rube Goldberg, or Randolph Hearst have the honor of presenting to American journalism the author of *I Am a City Editor, But I Always Called Them Sir,* and *Cholera, Goodbye—Your Medics Making Moslems Merry*

Again. The honor fell at last to a King Features executive whose daughter had been sprung by my father from a Baltimore drunk tank. This man assigned me to the *American Weekly,* the Hearst Sunday supplement whose best correspondents had been distinguishing themselves with their coverage of Hollywood and Transylvania. For fifty years, the *American Weekly* had been supplying a semi-literate nation with everything it needed to know about movie stars and vampire bats.

A few months after I had joined the *Weekly* staff, however, I was given a chance to write about a horror that my own father had been able to bring to an end in perhaps the greatest story of his career, one that should have brought to him a second Pulitzer Prize. From time to time since 1940, small homemade bombs had been discovered in public places throughout New York. Early in 1956, after two bombs had been found at Consolidated Edison plants and panic was growing popular, my father suggested to his publisher that the *Journal-American* print an open letter asking this Mad Bomber to surrender to the newspaper in exchange for psychiatric and legal help. He sounded like the kind of man who would have been a *Journal* reader and he was: the front-page letters brought printed replies whose fingerprints were traced by New York police.

"I'm proud of you, Poop," I told him one night after he had casually dazzled me with a letter from his pathological pen pal. "Who else could have established such a wonderful rapport with a lunatic?"

"Oh, the bedbugs read us, all right," he said with a smile. "But there's something you'd better learn, my

friend: half the people in this world are nuts. I've got reporters who aren't as sane as this guy."

When the Mad Bomber finally gave himself up, he
turned out to be a meek tubercular man of fifty-three
named George Metesky, who had simply wanted to blow
up the Consolidated Edison Company, a mission that made
him not insane but merely a little ahead of his time.

The story of the capture of the Mad Bomber was suf-
ficiently sensational for the *American Weekly,* which assigned me to write it for Bob Considine to sign. In a moving plea for identity, I said to my editor, "Why not let *me*
sign it instead of Considine? Wouldn't it be great to have
a son writing a story like this about his own *father?*"

"No," he said. "You have no name."

"But everybody thinks that I'm my father, so it would
almost be a first-person piece."

"Ralph, we're lucky that Considine has agreed to sign
this."

"I'm glad he can find the time," I said.

"I appreciate your disappointment," my editor said, "but
he's a very promotable name. And I think one Schoenstein is enough."

One Schoenstein is enough.

My father had kept telling me to carry on his name,
but now a message was coming through to find another
name to haul, a message I'd be hearing soon again. A few
days after I had carried on the name of Considine, I was
given a piece by H. Allen Smith on which a note from the
editor said: *Ralph—Please make this funny.—EVH*

Here was the work of one of America's most famous

humorists and the only thing it needed was for someone to make it funny. It was at this moment that I learned the only absolute truth I know: God may be in His heaven but absurdity rules the world.

As I rewrote H. Allen Smith from the depths of my anonymity, I discovered that I liked to write humor; and I got my chance to do more of it when the editor asked me to write a story for Walter Winchell about how Americans should cherish their right to vote. Since Winchell himself had never voted, the story was like an ode to orgasms signed by Pius XII. It was my third assignment to ghost in what was becoming for me an endless literary Halloween.

"Well, at least I'm Jewish again," I said to my father after telling him about the Winchell job. "Maybe I can make it back to Schoenstein in stages. In fact, we've got an Einstein piece in the house that could use a few laughs."

"This Winchell piece'll do you some good," my father said.

"How?" I said. "Nobody knows I'm writing it—not even Winchell. He's so crazy that he thinks he's doing it himself."

"Don't worry, I'll spread the word around. I know everybody—*you* know that. And spreading this one'll be a pleasure 'cause I'm still mad at that bastard Winchell for not running a line about your birth in his column."

"You should have let me write it," I said.

As the weeks went by, I grew more anxious to do stories that had started in my unpromotable mind. One afternoon while rewriting a piece that had been sloppily written by Pearl S. Buck, I suddenly said to myself, *My God, I'm ghosting the Nobel Prize!* There was no greater achievement for a ghost, except perhaps to punch up the Gospel According to St. Mark. Having arrived at my spectral peak, I decided to leave the *American Weekly* and try to do some freelance writing under the unlikely name of Ralph Schoenstein.

Once again I repaired to that East End terrace for a solemn session with Paul Schoenstein, the man who already had guided my career into ludicrous obscurity.

"*Freelancing?*" he said as if he were saying "male prostitute." "Poop, I can't tell you how important it is to keep on getting a weekly check. I've always had one—two in fact when the paper cut my salary in the Depression. I worked on the *Amsterdam News* at night, the only white man on a paper full of jigs."

I had never been able to teach my father that a jig was only a dance, just as I could never have taught the blacks with whom he had fought on the Harlem streets that my father's nickname was not Hey Kike.

"Well, I'd still like to try freelancing," I said. "Maybe I'll even take a crack at a newspaper column somewhere."

"What paper?" he said with concern.

"Don't worry, not yours. My vocabulary isn't small enough. Maybe the *Telegram* or the *Post.*"

"Out of the question. I can't have my son working for the opposition, for somebody like Dolly Schiff. Your name is Schoenstein, you know."

"No, it's Winchell, Considine, Smith, Pearl Buck, and *Paul* Schoenstein."

"Well, I still can't have you working for the other papers."

"Okay, then I'll have to lower my sights and work for you."

"Very funny. You know, of course, that I couldn't have my own son working for me."

"Let's see . . ." I said. " I can't work for the *Journal* and I can't work for the other afternoon papers and the *Times* doesn't have a column for me this week . . . Gee, it's really great to have a father in the business. It opens all the doors—in Cincinnati."

"Look, Poop," he said, "you simply have to understand my position. I'm a guy who—"

"Oh, I *know*," I bitterly said. "And I'll bet *your* father was never able to do this for you: block you from every place you wanted to work."

"Goddammit, will you *listen* to me! I'm in a very sensitive *position* down there! I'm the only Jew running a Hearst city desk and I will *not* have anyone accusing me of favoring my own son! So stop being a goddam *fool!*"

I said nothing for a few seconds while he looked out at the river with clenched molars and fists. Although terrified by his temper again, I was also savoring the ironies of his misplaced pride, for the Hearst organization was a shrine to nepotism: dozens of dimwitted relatives filled spots that professionals could have held; but for all his Superman-ish bluster, all his ebullience as Mister New York, my father still felt that he never belonged in this distinguished fraternity of free riders.

"Poop, I'm sorry I blew my cork," he said.

"That's okay," I said. "I don't mind working in Yokohama. I know a few people there. And maybe they've had penicillin by now."

He didn't laugh, for he was into his repetitious litany of remorse. Nobody since the Inquisition has apologized with my father's zeal.

"No, I'm really sorry," he said. "You know this lousy Hungarian temper of mine."

"With all those lousy tempers," I said, trying to lighten the confessional tone, "I wonder why Hungary never wins a war."

"Poop, please forgive me. Okay?"

"Three Hail Marys and you're clean," I said, squirming with uneasiness and wondering if all those other Hungarians went from rage to repentance with the maddening speed of Paul Schoenstein.

A few weeks after we had played this scene, I found the foreign employment that my father had dreamed about for me: the *Newark Star-Ledger* took a chance on a column of mine called "Doubletake," which satirized the news. My father and I were working on opposite sides of the Hudson River now and we were two different people at last: in a big red poster that the *Star-Ledger* put on its trucks, I was spelled RALPH SHOENSTEIN.

"I'm very proud of you," he said.

His pride in me was so automatic that he would have

been proud if I had told him that I had just deflowered a nun. He would have said, "I admire hard work."

As the *Journal-American's* Assistant Managing Editor now, my father was still pouncing on the big stories, while I was toying with the little ones. Although he was in his fifties when we began our journalistic tale of two cities, he was still the eager newsboy who had sold papers at the subway stations at the age of twelve, the year he started earning money so he could buy his own cigarettes. "I've got a big one," he would tell me urgently when he found a story like the quiz-show scandal: a contestant came to him and told of a fix and my father ran a series that caused a Congressional investigation of TV. "Jesus, television is as crooked as our circulation department," he had said to me.

When I began looking for laughter in Newark, my father was still the man *Newsweek* had described this way in 1948:

. . . In its cavernous East River-front office, the paper's cocky Pulitzer-Prize City Editor, Paul Schoenstein, pasted more clippings in his bulging "Scoop Book" and assigned a flying squad of reporters and photo men to bleed out every angle . . . Let it latch onto an exposé and the brassy *Journal-American* will rip in like a mongoose attacking a cobra, jabbing again and again until its story falls limp and exhausted.

As I had done since I was a boy, I continued to visit that cavernous river-front office on South Street, where my father and the other mongooses prowled around in search of snakes; and it was during those visits that I returned to being just Paul's Kid again.

I would always find him there because he was afraid to leave for lunch: he knew that the President of the United States could be shot at noon and the President of the Hearst Corporation could need matinee tickets at 12:45. And so he sat at that city desk for nine or ten hours every day, a cigarette burning before him, a black grease pencil in his hand, and his white sleeves neatly rolled halfway up; and he would keep reading the incoming news and the mind-rotting columnists of Hearst. In between telephone calls, he would read Walter Winchell's hymns to himself and Louella Parsons's attempts at English and Igor Cassini's kisses on the backsides of the rich; and he would read a critic named Rose Pelswick, who liked every film she ever saw because she always got in free, and a philosopher named Westbrook Pegler, who liked to mug Eleanor Roosevelt in print, and a fellow Cro-Magnon named George Sokolsky, who felt that World War II was not a black-and-white affair; and on top of all this numbing prose were the editorials that kept coming out for Douglas Mac-Arthur and dogs and that also congratulated God for being a part of the American team.

My father's political philosophy was the pursuit of the weekly check; and he also knew that this collection of hacks and flacks and goons did not precisely form a publication of distinction; but he also knew that he ran the paper as a kind of journalistic Salvation Army. While he sat there each day reading the poison, press agentry, and pap, while the rewrite men were feeding him the news from around the world, he was constantly waiting for that cry of help—from a man who hated Con Edison, from a woman who faked adulteries, or from the father of a dying child.

When I got off the elevator on the *Journal-American's* sixth floor, I was always greeted by a security guard who matched the ambiance of the place: a half-witted, half-sober old Irishman whom my father could have taken as a deduction on his income-tax return. And there were others in that building who siphoned off my father's cash: some were charity cases and some were gentlemen of sport.

"Every third guy in the joint is a bookie," my father often said to me. "They put out the paper on the side."

There was, in fact, so much off-track betting in the Journal-American building that a zealous young assistant district attorney once told the police to make a raid. When District Attorney Frank Hogan called his friend Paul to enjoy a laugh about these new horizons in crime, my father said, "I'm sorry you called off the raid, Frank. I had thirty reporters on the scene."

After I had passed this old Irishman and entered the enormous city room, I moved aimlessly about the most wondrous place I had ever seen, gazing as if for the first time at the galleys and headsets and spikes, hearing the never stale rhythms of the typewriters and wire-service machines, and looking for the latest photos of tits on the walls of the paper that began the Milk Fund. My father would finally summon me to his desk, always as if he were calling a cab; and when I reached him, he always annoyed me with the same piece of social advice: "Go over and say hello to Eddie and Rock and Walter and Red." It was Paul Schoenstein's maddening manners course; but when he accompanied me the chore turned to fun because he had a camaraderie with these men that was full of affectionate abuse.

"Hi-ya, Ralphie," Max Kase, the sports editor, would say. "I like that column you're doing, kid."

"Who's reading it to you?" my father would say.

"This apple certainly fell far from the tree," Max would reply. "Are you sure that this bum is your father, Ralphie? I mean, I know he's got kids all over Hawaii, but— Jeeesus!"

This sudden religious outpouring had been caused by a punch to Max's shoulder that sent him reeling toward his desk; and now I knew that his fist would reply in this little game of shot-for-shot that my father often played to give black-and-blue tokens to the men he loved the most. I didn't see all of his matches, of course, but he lost none of those at which I was the entire ringside crowd, for he was clearly the strongest Jewish City Editor in the Western World. In fact, one of the *Journal-American* legends was the way he once had disarmed a man who had burst into the office with a knife, probably someone who'd come to make a point to Westbrook Pegler.

The responses to my column in Newark were weaker than those that Pegler drew and I felt no closer to conquering the beckoning RCA sign. The closest I came to these letters that year was the night I took a marvelous girl named Judy Greenspan to the roof of the RCA Building and told her she had to marry me. Looking down at Manhattan, I said to her, "Someday all of this will be yours." I knew that a similar view of Newark would never have made her agree to spend her life spelling Schoenstein on the telephone.

"I'm getting married," I told my father the following day.

"I just hope you find a girl like your mother," he replied as if writing the lyric of a new Irish song.

"I've *found* one," I told him, "and she's different."

"I'd be in the gutter if it weren't for your mother."

"Poop, I'm getting *married*," I said, trying to break through his salute to my mother's missionary work.

"Hey, that's great, Poop; that's really great."

"I may take *her* into the gutter, but she's the kind of girl who'll go. She's passing up a millionaire for me, which means she's crazy enough for this family."

"She doesn't need a millionaire when she's got a Schoenstein," he said. "We'll get Durante for the wedding. And maybe Frank Sinatra, too."

"But just forget about having it at Yankee Stadium," I said to him.

About a month after our engagement, Judy came to a dinner party that my parents adorned with some Hearst officials for whom my father felt a touching blend of loyalty and fear. It was a feeling that long before had driven me in the opposite political direction, the way that a minister's piety supposedly opens his daughter's legs.

"They're a bunch of right-wing bastards," I told my father on the day of the party while he agonized over which of two new Brooks Brothers shirts he should wear.

"Now look, I've *told* you," he sharply replied. "He whose bread I eat, his praises I sing."

I had always preferred his singing of "The Anniversary Song" to his hallelujah for Hearst, no matter how hard he tried to make me understand his loyalty to these men whose rampant Americanism exalted babies, dogs, and Chiang Kai-shek.

"Okay, I'll kiss their rings," I said.

"You don't have to be a goddam wise guy about it," he replied with a jaw that was starting to tighten up. "Just watch your political cracks. Is that picture of Stalin still in your room?"

"Jesus, I took that down *years* ago. Don't you pay attention to *anything* besides the paper?"

"Okay, mister, that's enough."

"*God*, I hate the way you have to grovel before those guys."

"Your father doesn't grovel before *anyone*. And they're the top men in the whole organization."

"No, *you're* the top man," I said, "and they should be grateful to have someone like you."

And then, with a guilty little smile, he held his thumb and index finger about half an inch apart, a familiar sign that meant I was now to bring him a shot of gin, one to be smuggled past my mother as if it were a quarter of a glass of water.

"Get me one," he said. "Okay?"

For the first couple of hours, the party was as festive as applying for a loan, with my father paying slightly tipsy homage to the giants of journalism who were managing to dismantle the world's largest publishing company. The *Daily Mirror*, the *American Weekly*, and the International News Service were already gone; Hearst newspapers around the country were saying "Rosebud" year after year; and the empire that so long had been devoted to the Christian way was now seeking salvation in the Gospel According to Helen Gurley Brown, whose *Cosmopolitan* was proving that manhunting was as salable as the Spanish-American War.

King Features Syndicate, however, was still in business, dispensing comics and Commie control. Moments after the meal had ended and the guests had moved to the living room, the Syndicate's president, a pink-cheeked, cold-eyed man in his early sixties, said to me, "Your father showed me that column you're doing for the Newark paper, Paul, and I think you're on your way to being another Bob Considine."

It was hard to keep from telling him that this was a trip I had already made; but I had promised my father that I would treat these men as if they deserved respect.

After calling me a present Paul Schoenstein and a future Bob Considine, the King Features leader went on to explore even richer critical depths by saying, "But let me give you one tip, lad. Never start a column with the word 'recently.' You see, nobody knows when recently was."

I was barely able to make a reply, for I was moved to near dumbness by the stunning absurdity of this aesthetic point from a man whose most literate feature was Donald Duck.

Suddenly, about ten o'clock, I looked toward the foyer of the apartment to see my father with his arm around the wife of one of the men and his fingers squeezing her starboard breast. I wanted to think that he was doing exercises to strengthen his hand, but I had to face the fact that I had caught him doing fieldwork for *Cosmopolitan* and I was so discomfited by the sight that I quickly retreated to the piano, where I began to play, hoping that my father's hand was moving from the milk to the gin.

A few minutes later, after running through some Rodgers and Kern, I found myself doing a song for Judy that I had sung in my high-school days, when I had been the most politically active child since Joan of Arc. In memory of Henry Wallace's 1948 campaign, I sang:

> *Everyone loves Wallace,*
> *Friendly Henry Wallace,*
> *Everyone wants Wallace in the White House.*

As if yanked by strings, the heads of some of the Hearst men turned to me and their expressions would have been the same if I had just suggested that a statue of Lenin be erected in Times Square. Now fully conscious of what I had done and properly horrified by it, I tried to play "You're a Grand Old Flag," but I suddenly couldn't remember the chords; and this same blankness kept me from doing "America" and "Over There." In fact, I seemed to have forgotten every song I'd ever known except "Oats Peas Beans and Barley Grow," but I was afraid that this one would sound like a musical portrait of Wallace's farm. I was now too flustered to perform any number other than "Chopsticks," which I quickly did to close my act in a subtle salute to Mao Tse-tung. As I left the piano, I was thankful that my father hadn't seemed to notice my little subversive serenade.

One of the people at that party was the *Journal-American*'s publisher, J. Kingsbury Smith, the latest in a series of publishers to whom my father had given lessons in how a newspaper was put out. A man who deliberated his moves, Smith waited six years and then gave me a call.

"Ralph, I'd like you to start writing 'Doubletake' for the *Journal-American*," he said.

"Does my father know about this?" I replied.

"*I'm* hiring you, not your father," he said. "I'll pay you fifty dollars for two columns a week."

In spite of this almost unnoticeable salary, I decided to let my wife and two young daughters shift for themselves and I accepted Smith's offer to bring my hobby to the *Journal-American*, where I would be the first New York columnist with a chance to write about his own food stamps.

And so here it was at last: my own column in the biggest

evening newspaper in the world; and the challenge there would be unique: to keep my father from reading it. By dinnertime, however, I had decided to reveal my good fortune to the man who unknowingly had become my boss.

"Poop, guess what happened today," I nervously said. "Joe Smith called me and asked me to do my column for the paper."

"*You called Joe Smith and asked—*"

"No, no, *he* called *me*—I *swear!*"

He was silent for a couple of seconds; and then he took a deep drag of his cigarette and said to me in a cloud of smoke, "I don't know . . . I just don't know . . . Two Schoensteins on one paper . . ."

"You're right," I said. "You'll have to go. But you may still have a shot at the *Amsterdam News*—as long as you don't tell 'em you're white."

Without a smile, he said, "I'll have to be very tough on you. You'll have to be twice as good."

"Twice as good as *what?*" I said, suddenly finding my temper unleashed. "Pegler and Parsons and Pelswick and the *rest* of your know-nothing brigade? Twice as good as Jim *Bishop*, whose columns sound like *telegrams?* As Bugs *Baer*, who writes those jokes in *code?* As Burt Bacharach's poetic tips on how to remove *spaghetti* stains? Or Jack O'Brian's mile-long sentences, which are so garbled that you—that you could make a *puzzle* out of them and see if anyone can find the *verb!* Jesus, Poop, most of the paper isn't as well written as a goddam McGuffey *Reader!*"

"You finished your speech?" he said.

"Yeah. A pretty good one, don't you think? And I left out Serge Fliegers, whose stuff is so pompous that it sounds like letters from Peter the Great."

"Now you listen to me, Mister Mencken. I don't give a *shit* about any of them. *You've* got my name and I'm the *editor*. People will be pointing fingers at *us!*"

"But you've—"

"So stop being *stupid* and start using your *brains.*"

"But you've already *got* families down there. Jim Kilgallen and Dorothy, and Bugs Baer and Atra, and—"

"Okay, now let's talk about *you*," he said. "Just make the column as good as you can and stay away from the valentines to Henry Wallace."

"What do you mean?" I said.

"You remember that party a few years ago—with all the Hearst brass?"

I smiled sheepishly. "The song I sang. You know, I thought you didn't hear it."

"I heard you, Paderewski. I decided not to make an issue of it."

"Well, it's a little late, but thanks," I said, wanting to hug him and tell him that I forgave him too for his sexual freelancing that night, that he had my permission to squeeze any damn thing he wanted. "I didn't play it badly, but it really needed your voice."

"Those Commie songs aren't in my key."

"Poop, about the column . . . I promise I won't embarrass you. It'll be *George* Wallace for me from now on. And I'll never start a column with 'recently.' "

"What are you talking about?"

"A private joke."

"Well, none of that in the column. Don't make it too sophisticated."

"But, Poop, this is *New York.*"

"Where the people are schmucks like everywhere else," he said, and the sign on the RCA Building began to dim.

The following day, I told my editor at the *Newark Star-Ledger* about my move across the river.

"So your old man got you a column," he said.

"Yes," I replied. "It's the least he could do."

5

AN APPLE NOT FAR
FROM THE TREE

The composing room of the *Journal-American* had not set
any writing of mine since the spring of 1945, when my
father had pushed his pride in me to the ludicrous edge by
having his printers pull a hundred galleys of a four-minute
play that I had written to explain the building of the
Panama Canal to the seventh grade, a play with the mys-
tical title of *Bully, My Boys, Let's Charge!* Of course, perhaps my father knew that Mr. Hearst would have been
happy to see his flagship paper printing this stirring salute
to Teddy Roosevelt's All-American conquest of mosquitoes,
heat, and property rights:

COLONEL THEODORE "TEDDY" ROOSEVELT: Now hear this! I want
    the Panama Canal dug *here!*
DR. GORGAS: (*Pointing to a fever chart*) But Colonel Roosevelt,
    there is yellow fever here.
COLONEL THEODORE "TEDDY" ROOSEVELT: I really don't care! The
    fever may be yellow but *Americans* never are! Bully, my
    boys, let's dig!
COLONEL GOETHALS: (*Pointing to a map on the wall of the hut*)

But Colonel Roosevelt, we don't *own* Panama. I think that we should buy it first.

COLONEL THEODORE "TEDDY" ROOSEVELT: I really don't care what we own! America has a destiny to help poor people all over the world with new canals. And so I say bully, my boys, let's charge!

This placement of the building of the Panama Canal in the middle of the Spanish-American War was a representative work of art from the formative years of Citizen Ralph. And now my father no doubt was yearning to again be printing my cockeyed rhapsodies to imperial America instead of my looks at a loony America that made him fearful of offending half of the bar at "21."

My first column managed to get through because I was wise enough to spoof the Russians, who didn't advertise in the *Journal-American*. I was so elated after turning the column in that I went to watch the presses run it off, feeling the same awe that I had felt when I was six and the giant roaring rollers were my private Niagara Falls.

However, I pushed my luck too far and wrote a second column two days later. It was about the Pan Am Building, an Orwellian nightmare that had risen like a concrete weed to choke off Grand Central Station, where my father had launched me for camp on many happy summer nights.

"I can't run this piece," my father said. "Pan Am is a big advertiser with us and you should've been aware of that."

"But that's the *airline*, not the *building*," I said. "Even *your* readers know the difference. I mean, the airline goes to Paris and the building stays right here. Of course, the building *could* use throw-up bags."

"Look, smartass," he said, "you're making fun of the name Pan Am and I can't take a chance on something like that. I *told* you to lay off the advertisers."

"But dammit the *building* doesn't advertise! They're not offering package flights in the *elevator*. Jesus, Poop, you've got to be *kidding* about killing the column for a reason like that!"

Turning away in disgust, I saw a reporter named Walter Stern, a jovial man who had driven me home from Stuyvesant High School every day for three years because my father was deeply religious about keeping his family out of the subway. Going over to this ex-chauffeur, I said, "Walter, will you please tell your editor the difference between the Pan Am airline and the Pan Am Building?"

"You mean he doesn't know?" said Walter with a grin as my father rose from his desk and approached us. "I *knew* he left school in the second grade—that's the grade that Hungarians just can't get—but even a backward Hungarian should know . . . well, tell him that the airline goes *vrooommm* and the building goes—son of a *bitch!*"

Walter might have told me more about the difference between jets and cement but he was busy falling into a desk where my father happened to have knocked him.

"Ralphie, from now on, just ask me the time," said Walter as he slowly went vertical again while rubbing his arm.

"Walter, I would dearly love to hear more of your rich

storehouse of knowledge," my father said with the dead-pan expression he always took on when he was acting like a nine-year-old. "Perhaps you'd like to lecture on the land-fills of Hackensack that you'll be doing a series on."

"Ralphie, you're on your own," said Walter, moving away. "He won't hit *you*."

My father was, however, giving me a stronger blow than a mere right cross; but I was much too close to this city-desk Dempsey to fight back with any force, for it was hard to make a ringing defense of freedom of the press against the oppression of the tyrant who had squeezed my orange juice. If only my copy could have been handled with the respect that had been given to the Mad Bomber's.

My replacement column sailed right through, and so did the one that followed it, because neither the Mafia nor Bugs Bunny were important friends of Mr. Hearst; but then I did a piece on labor that moved my father to in-quire, "What the hell is wrong with you? It bothers you that the paper isn't on strike?"

"You think this column'll start a *strike?*" I said incredu-lously.

"No, because I'm not running it. Go knock out another."

"Now just a big fat minute," I said, my golden tongue beginning to shine. "*Considine* hit the unions last week. Even Jimmy *Cannon* writes about them. How come you never kill *their* stuff?"

"Because they're not my sons," he said, taking a ciga-rette from a case that I had given to him that said:

To Poop

Greatest editor
Finest father
Nicest guy

And now I wanted to amend the inscription by adding: *Or none of the above.*

"Look, all I want is *equal treatment,*" I said to the former Mister Fixit, who was now fixing me with a different style. "Just treat me the same way you treat everybody *else.*"

"I can't," he said. "I have to be tougher on you."

I turned and presented my biceps to him, unable to suppress a smile, for against Paul Schoenstein I had a short aggravation span.

"Would you settle for just rupturing a vein or two?" I said.

He laughed and then took a telephone call from a Japanese urologist whom he had saved from internment camp at the beginning of World War II. The urologist had felt such gratitude that he seemed unable to wait for a chance to remove my father's prostate as a gift and perhaps even have it bronzed for him. Overhearing the call, I found myself wishing for the first time in my life that I was not Paul Schoenstein's son. Maybe then I would have been able to know the unqualified generosity that he showed to drinking companions and delivery boys. Blood may have been thicker than water to him, but it still lacked the consistency of gin.

"How would you like to take my place as Paul Schoenstein's son?" I asked Jimmy Cannon after telling the censorship story to him.

"I know the problem well," he said. "That's why all the Roosevelt and Churchill kids are idiots. It's better if your old man is a bum—which yours is, by the way; but he's also the sweetest man in town."

In the months that followed, the sweetest man in town killed my columns with a flair that belonged on *Pravda*. The record for the most columns killed by my father had previously been held by Westbrook Pegler for a series of think pieces proving that Eleanor Roosevelt was responsible for the Second World War, the loss of China, and the increase in shoplifting; but Pegler's record was topped by me as my list of forbidden subjects grew until I began to pine for the days when I had been free to be Pearl Buck.

In addition to suffering a censorship designed to protect my family name, I also discovered at this time that my scarlet letter was still aglow. A book of mine came out and a critic at the *Times* named Herbert Mitgang said that it contained "the collective sound of the humor columnists at the *Journal-American*." In support of this remarkable opinion, he made five mistakes about the book in a 350-word review, revealing that either his reading speed was too high or his IQ was too low. The review, however, was not without its rewards because collecting *Times* mistakes had been my hobby since I was nine and this was striking a mother lode.

My father plays the piano in a whorehouse, teacher, I

heard myself saying again as I brooded over Herbert Mitgang's review and wondered what the collective sound of the *Journal-American*'s humor columnists could be. There were only three of us—Louella Parsons, Bugs Baer, and myself—and our styles were hardly a harmony.

"I'll *crucify* the bastard!" he said about Mitgang as he drove his car up the East River Drive.

"What can you do to him?" I said. "Keep his name out of the paper the way you kept out Orson Welles? You guys really taught Welles a lesson. You restricted his fame to just the planet earth."

I knew that the only punishment the *Journal* could have given to Mitgang would have been to support him for public office.

"That goddamned *Times* stuffed shirt," said my father, stepping on the accelerator as if it were Mitgang's face.

"I'm sending a letter to the *Times*," I said, "listing all the things he found that aren't in the book."

"Be careful what you say."

"Are you *kidding?*" I cried.

"Well, you'll be signing Schoenstein in the *Times* and—"

"*Jesus,* Poop, you wanna crucify him *carefully?* Okay, I'll use very clean nails."

Suddenly the siren of a police car sounded and my father looked around; but this time the story was Paul Schoenstein.

"Okay, license and registration, mister," said the cop who made us stop.

"Officer, I'm the editor of the *Journal-American*," my

father said, producing not his license but his working
press card.

"You *are?*" said the cop as if he had met Joe DiMaggio.
"It's my *favorite paper.*"

"Mine, too," said my father and the two of them laughed.

"I love Jack O'Brian and Prince Valiant and Winchell—
and Kilgallen, I think she's terrific."

"She's a helluva reporter," my father said.

"And George Sokolsky and the Katzenjammer Kids,"
said the cop, naming the paper's principal pro-Germanic
wing.

For the next five minutes, a *Journal-American* fan club
held a meeting in the right lane of the East River Drive
just below the UN. I kept waiting for the cop to get to
my column, but I seemed to be the only one he didn't like.
I was probably more popular with meter maids.

"So you're really the *editor* of the *Journal-American,*"
said the cop. "Your paper's been really good to the police
force, you know."

"We're very much in favor of the police force," said my
father in a tone so grandly paternal that I was expecting
him to ask the cop if he wanted any parking tickets fixed.

"My gosh, I'm holdin' you up," said the cop. "You're
probably rushin' to a story right now."

"It may be a big one," said my father, somewhat over-
rating the news value of the goulash he was about to eat.

"I'll getcha through this bottleneck. Follow me."

Watching my father accelerate behind his police escort,

I wondered if I would ever have the style to turn a pinch into a parade.

A couple of minutes later, we were about to leave the highway for home when my father decided to visit his favorite reporter, who had been taken to Mount Sinai Hospital.

"I want to make sure that Syd is getting all the whiskey he needs," my father said.

When we entered the hospital, however, a receptionist told us that the reporter was allowed to have no visitors now.

"That's correct," said my father. "I'm Dr. Travers."

"And I'm Dr. Schlesinger," I heard myself say as my heart slammed on a bone whose name I should have known.

"Oh, I'm *sorry*, doctors," the receptionist said. "Please go right up."

I had done it! The son of Dr. Bullshit was launched! Of course, being Dr. Schlesinger at Mount Sinai was a long way from being a police inspector at a heavyweight championship fight, but at least my dormant genes for deception suddenly had come alive and the man who had given them to me was delighted.

As the elevator began to take us up, my father said, "Hey, that was *good*," with the kind of pride that Fagin felt when Oliver brought back his first pocketbook.

"Poop, this is *crazy*," I said. "They're liable to ask us to *operate*."

I had never felt a strong desire to follow my father into the impostor game; I would have settled for impersonating an average *Journal* columnist; and now I was a doctor in alliance with this marvelous maddening man who gave commands to cops and hospitals but bowed to anybody named Hearst.

As we approached the reporter's room, my courage crumbled and I wanted to go on the hospital's public address and say, "In case you might have misunderstood, Dr. Schlesinger is only a *Ph.D.*—and it's just in *sociology*."

The man we were sneaking in to see, Syd Boehm, was the man that my father had planted in Camp Siegfried, a Long Island unit of the German-American Bund, to get the story of how certain New Yorkers had lost track of who the good guys were in the early days of World War II. After impersonating a Bundist for a couple of weeks one summer, Syd was ready to bring his story back when his fellow campers discovered that he was not only a *Journal* reporter but also Jewish. Either would have been enough for disqualification from the Bund; but being both entitled Syd to be evicted with a broken jaw.

Sending a reporter out to become a sunshine fascist was the kind of comic-book journalism my father seemed to have invented when he became the *Journal's* City Editor. Long before it was common for papers to do undercover work, my father was Hearst's busy gardener, planting reporters everywhere from insane asylums to Nazi camps.

"I'll bet you would have planted a man in the manger," I once said to him.

Smiles from the best-dressed man at ringside
and the Mona Lisa, his son

OVERLEAF
My second home, the *Journal-American* city room, under the direction
of the City Editor, who sits in front of the steampipe in a dark tie and
a shirt that is just a little whiter than the rest

America's busiest Other Woman, and the man to whom she confessed that most divorces in New York State were based on make-believe

After the capture of the Mad Bomber, *Journal-American* publisher Seymour Berkson points to the story while the Bomber's pen pal, Paul Schoenstein, and other editors look on

With Harry Truman,
to whom he probably said,
"I'm Mister New York"

With the shortest mayor in his collection, Fiorello La Guardia,
and *Journal-American* Editor-in-Chief William Curley

With the jewel of his mayoral collection, Jimmy Walker,
an alternate Mister New York

With John V. Lindsay,
just a casual friend,
for Episcopal mayors
were hard to collect

I am shaking part of
the hand of another
of his friends

With the girl who removed
him from the gutter

Giving a lift to a child
he felt eclipsed the
Infant Jesus

During a sacred moment
at my bar mitzvah

Also at my bar mitzvah:
a few solemn words upon coming of age just before a station break

They're either too young or too old at Mitchell Field
as World War II begins

I am biting my lip to keep from accidentally talking
while he is on the air

Is he batting a baseball or killing a snake?

The fighting corporal who almost became the son of G. David Schine

Mister New York

"Sure, Guy Richards, our Yalie," he replied. "I could have passed him off as a wise man. But the resurrection—that would have been tough. Of course, it was a morning-paper story anyway."

He sat reminiscing now with Syd about the days of *Front Page* adventures, while I wandered to the window of the room and looked dreamily at the western sky. The city whose lights were coming on was no longer the city where my father had appointed himself as Mister New York, for half of these lights were to drive away thugs instead of to glisten above the streets where my father and Jimmy Walker, with carnations in their lapels, took sentimental strolls. Double-decker buses were gone, sky-view cabs had been replaced by checkered armored cars, newsboys had given way to boy muggers, newsstands were less interested in headlines than giving head, and the streets no longer looked like a giant set for Fred Astaire, although you had to move like Astaire if you wanted to keep yourself out of the shit.

"If Mr. Hearst had stepped in this stuff," my father once told me while wiping his shoe, "we might've been in *favor* of vivisection."

I was gazing now at the towers across the city on Central Park West, where I had ended many evenings as a boy in attempts to make contact with middle-class breasts. Blouses fell more easily now, but the city around them had fallen, too, and I suddenly envied my father for knowing New York when it had still been Bagdad-on-the-Hudson: when the lyrics of "Manhattan" still made sense, when the subway was a nickel's worth of fun instead of a quarter's worth of anxiety, when Sixth Avenue was full of lively pubs instead of sixty-story monuments, and when there was fiercer fighting inside Madison Square Garden than out on the street.

A few days after our visit to Syd, my father became the *Journal-American*'s Managing Editor, a promotion that moved him to give me a copy of the new staff box, on which he wrote:

> *Poop—*
>
> *A far cry from Lenox Avenue*
>
> *Love,*
>
> *Poop* ·

And now it looked as though I was going to be a far cry from the *Journal-American* because Joe Smith suddenly decided to cut my column to one appearance a week, relieving me of the pressure to find such subjects as Father's Day, hay fever, and Red Chinese to satirize. I hardly glowed with satisfaction to know that at the age of thirty-two I was making twenty-five dollars a week, slightly less than what I could have made by playing the guitar in a bus terminal; and I would have had more artistic freedom in the terminal, too.

"Is Ralph working yet, or is he still writing?" my wife's college roommate said to her.

"He does a column for the *Journal-American*," Judy replied as though revealing a secret.

My decline was progressing at a lively pace when Dorothy Kilgallen died, Jack O'Brian took her column, and the paper needed a critic for TV. The job was given to a reporter named Atra Baer, whose *Journal-American* father, Bugs Baer, did not share my father's feeling about keeping relatives obscure.

"But five pieces a week will be plenty for Atra," said Joe Smith to my father, "so suppose we give Ralph a crack at the TV reviewing for Saturday."

My father felt this was a fine idea because the Saturday edition of the *Journal* was read only in the composing room. He would feel as though he were printing my play about the Panama Canal again.

The following day, Joe Smith announced that the *Journal-American's* new Saturday television critic would be Ralph Schoenstein, the sometime author of "Doubletake." And then the head of the *Journal-American* unit of the New York Newspaper Guild announced that if I became the Saturday critic, the paper would be shut down by a strike because I was a freelance writer and not a member of the Guild.

"It's the most chickenshit thing I've ever heard," said my father, wishing that I were safely back in Newark or Stuyvesant.

"And you're going to *fight* it—right?" I said.

"Well, the Guild is tough, you know. And a strike . . ."

"But it's *ridiculous!* For one column a *week?* I tell you, they're just *bluffing.*"

"Well, I'm a pretty good poker player myself."

"And you've got all the cards. Poop, I *know* the men would never vote for such a stupid strike. Some of them used to drive me to *school.*"

"Just let me handle it," my father said.

The moment that every boy dreams about, the moment when he sends his father into battle with the cry "Go *get* 'im, Pop!", had now become mine; but Mister New York was out of office, Mister Fixit had lost his tools, and Clark Kent stepped out of his clothes to reveal himself as Neville Chamberlain. I watched with rage and disbelief as my father yielded to the Guild and replaced me with a staff reporter. The loss of the column, however, was the less painful of the two blows I received, for reviewing TV in the Saturday *Journal* was like doing the weather report in the *Times*. What hurt much more was having to finally admit to myself that my father couldn't lick every other father on the block if one of them happened to run a newspaper or a newspaper guild. My boyhood idol had, of course, shown me feet of clay many times before; but now I saw knees of Play-Doh, too.

From the vantage point of the funk from which I saw things after being fired before my first review appeared, it seemed to me that my future in journalism was answering Walter Winchell's mail. I was about to give up "Doubletake" and seek honest employment on the docks when the unthinkable came to pass: the *Journal-American* folded and my father beat me to the unemployment line. He had spent forty-two years on this one newspaper and suddenly he had no place to go after making my mother's orange juice.

"Poop, all you have to do is go over to the *News* or the *Times* or the *Post*," I said. "I mean, how many Pulitzer Prize winners do you think those papers have?"

"Everybody on the *Times* has a Pulitzer Prize but the copy boys," he said. "That's why it meant so much when I won it with Hearst. Anyway, they wouldn't go for my style. I don't know how to cover chess."

"Okay, then the *News* or the *Post*."

"The *News* has a lot of good men there already," he said. "It's the best-edited paper in America. And I'd rather cut my throat than go to work for Dolly Schiff. She's a bitch on wheels. And even if she wasn't, the *Post* is still a piece of crap. Your paper at Stuyvesant was better."

He was silent for a moment and so was I, for I had run out of papers and was not about to suggest the *Newark Star-Ledger*.

"I'm sixty-four years old," he said, "so nobody's knocking down my door. But I can't complain; I've had a pretty good run. Especially for a guy who's really just a plodder —and could've ended up in jail. You know, there's an awful lot wrong with me."

To see him without his gaiety, his cockiness, and his adolescent élan was to see him as if he were naked; and I felt that something wonderful had gone out of my life.

"Are you *kidding?*" I said, trying to shore up his morale. "You're the greatest self-made man I've ever known."

"Well, I guess I've learned a couple of things since the Lindbergh case," he said with a little smile. "Did I ever tell you how I handled that one? I was Night City Editor at the time and the bulletin on the kidnapping got me so flustered that I sent every man in the office to Hopewell, New Jersey. It's a wonder I didn't send the elevator man to Hopewell too."

Not too long after my father and I had held this bittersweet exchange, he was given a reprieve from retirement and he found himself with another chance to sit behind the city desk. The *World Journal Tribune* was put together from the remains of three newspapers; and, true to its manner of creation, it had all the sparkle of a compost heap. Not only did this hybrid lack a style and point of view, but my father was trying to galvanize three separate staffs that had formed the uneasiest alliance since the Hitler-Stalin pact. The *Journal-American* people were jealous of those from the *Herald Tribune* because the people from the *Tribune* had houses in the Hamptons instead of lockers at Jones Beach; and the *Tribune* people felt that those from the *Journal* should have been properly placed on the *Police Gazette*. The only rapport between these two staffs was their common feeling that the people from the *World-Telegram* were schmucks.

The people my father cared about, those with great stories to reveal, never came to see him at the *World Journal Tribune* because someone in trouble does not confess to a newspaper that needs the last rites itself. The lifeless pages of this paper were a dreary contrast to the commanding ones that had filled the *Journal-American;* but my father, just one member of a committee of editors, was powerless to put his stamp on things, to inspire his reporters to go after anything more than other jobs.

When the *World Journal Tribune* began to print, I reappeared in my father's office, but now I wasn't working for him. I was a minor part of Clay Felker's *New York,* the paper's Sunday supplement, whose New Journalism gave a writer a choice of getting the facts or making them up.

"I *fired* men for writing less bullshit than Felker is running," my father said, dismayed by the turn that his business had taken. "Some of those Breslin and Sheehy pieces —they should be given fiction awards."

It was no longer my father's world. It was the world of an editor who planted reporters not in criminal rings but in chic saloons. Were a *New York* writer to have gotten the story of the German-American Bund, he would have waited for Fritz Kuhn to come and have a drink at Elaine's.

I used to stand near the city desk and watch Clay Felker question my father about the way to cover a story and the way to make up a page. Felker, however, was careful not to be seen with my father for more than just a few minutes at a time because he worshipped power and he sensed that my father was a deity deposed. And, of course, he was right: my father's punch had disappeared: both his connection to City Hall and his famous city-room right hand, which was barely breaking capillaries now. In fact, he no longer found it fun to play heavyweight champ with the men he loved. Shot-for-shot in my father's life had come to mean only swallows of gin.

By the fall of 1966, while the *World Journal Tribune* was still publishing the news of the week in review, I had lived a surrealistic adventure in which the White House had forced Doubleday to cancel the printing of a book I had written about Lyndon Johnson and his dogs. It was a harmless little book, for Johnson may not have known how to deal with anything that approached him on two legs, but he did trigger empathy in hounds. The overkill involved in the suppression of this book by a zealous flack named Elizabeth Carpenter drove me to write a story, *My Year in the White House Doghouse,* which captured the qualities of Lyndon Johnson that were starting to touch the American people: a folksy megalomania and an arrogance as big as all outdoors. I took the story to Felker, who decided to let it fill an entire issue of *New York.*

"But I'm afraid we'd better not show it to Kamm or Conniff or even your father," Felker said. "This paper has friends in the White House and we'd have trouble getting it through."

And so, in an episode as absurd as the one I had lived in Washington, I hid the biggest story I had ever written from my father, who was about to publish it. This was the system that I should have used for doing "Doubletake."

Although elated by the imminent appearance of my study of White House mental illness, I was also depressed by my disloyalty, for I was a conspirator against my own father. It was intoxicating to realize that at last I was on my own; but what rotten timing to have broken away at the moment my father was starting to die.

My Year in the White House Doghouse caused enough reaction for *Newsweek* to do a story on me with a veracity that my father envied. When *Time* had written a story about his capture of the Mad Bomber, the fiction rivaled a tax return and made the *Journal-American* sue and win a settlement out of court. If I had grown up responsible for the Spanish-American War, I wondered what guilt was carried by the sons of the editors of Luce. The sinking of the *Lusitania* perhaps?

The day after *Newsweek* had discussed me in a piece called "Shaggy Tale," my father took me to dinner at Toots Shor's. As a boy of ten in Toots Shor's I had met my father's friend Joe DiMaggio and the place was afterwards Oz to me; but as a man I had grown uneasy with its strained camaraderie, with the studied macho of men who seemed to be trying to recapture the mindlessness of their days at Alpha Delta Phi.

They stood two and three deep at a great round bar: the media men, the halfbacks, the actors, the salesmen, the flacks, and the fakes, and they lost themselves in booze and boy talk in America's plushest locker room. My father lacked their desire for deals, their knowledge of sports, and their three hours for lunch; and he always *lived* a good game of newspapering instead of talking one. It was, nonetheless, important to him to be hailed by this fraternity and to exchange insults with Toots Shor, the former bouncer who blessed you by calling you a bum.

"Here comes Toots," my father said that night after jumping up to greet Robert F. Wagner. The contact with Wagner was only a modest score on the scale of social prestige because he was a non-charismatic ex-Mayor; but my father didn't know Frank Gifford or Howard Cosell, who sat nearby; and old standbys of his like Tom Dewey and Jim Farley were no longer on the scene.

Shor stopped at our table primarily because my father grabbed his arm, but he was looking across the room. The "Hi-ya, Paul, ya crum bum" that I expected did not come.

"Toots, it's wonderful to see you," my father said as he stood up, with a deference in his manner that made me want to disappear. "You remember Ralph, of course."

Shor gave his hand to me as if I had told him I was an auditor from the IRS.

"Sure, hi-ya," he said, still looking away. My father could launch no affable insult because Toots Shor wasn't there.

"Wonderful to see you again, Tootsie," my father finally said as if saying goodbye to one of the Hearsts.

"You, too," said Shor. Whoever you are.

And then the big lovable bum moved on, having destroyed one of Jimmy Walker's two best friends on the very spot where my father and Walker had sat in the spotlight two decades before. I wanted to throw the ketchup at Shor, for a blow to his pride in front of his son was something my father didn't need.

"He's a sweetheart, that Tootsie," my father said, pretending it was still 1946; and then we went to sit with a press agent my father had spent twenty years avoiding. Still fawning over my father by reflex action, the press agent said to his son as we came to his table, "This is the legendary Paul Schoenstein."

The son, a man about thirty, instantly responded to the name. "Are you Ralph's father?" he said.

6

OCCASIONAL

LIFE WITH FATHER

My youngest daughter, now one year old, awoke at six in the crib where she had slept beneath a plaque that said:

Presented to
PAUL SCHOENSTEIN
New York Journal-American
For distinguished service to his
community in the field of journalism
PALL MALL AWARD

When she saw me, she smiled and said, "Daddy, Daddy," and began to bounce up and down; and then I kissed her cheek and carried her to the kitchen as the urine ran down my chest. I felt like a lamppost and yet I would not have traded this dousing for a dip in a pool. As I took off Lori's clothes in the sink and covered her tiny torso with kisses, I thought about my father, who sooner would have gone to bed with Dorothy Schiff than have peeled a dirty diaper from his baby girl. He lived in a time when men got pissed on at the office and let their wives be the targets at home; and now I was sad to think

111

that he had never known a moment as sweet as this, for he was an openly loving and sensual man and should not have been stopped by the folly of machismo from sliding his soapy hands over someone who was smiling at him from a sink.

I thought of my father again while I was drying Lori with a towel, for I suddenly buried my face in the middle of her body and blew hard, producing a sound that a second-rate tuba student might have made; and I remembered once having seen my father, the noted Hungarian wet kisser, play my sister's stomach like this while my mother had done the diapering. The earthy noise of my solo made Lori explode with laughter, which I needed to fortify myself against the blows of the coming day. In a world where almost nothing made sense, a world where accident was routine, the joy of my children was not only the greatest pleasure I had ever known but also the best defense I could find against the absurdities of life.

The music I made with Lori was not always as crude as turning her tummy into a little wind instrument. A few hours earlier, at midnight, I had waltzed her around the kitchen while singing along with *The Marriage of Figaro,* moving Lori to sing along with me in a blend of the Metropolitan and the rotten that still managed to be sublime. I have learned that my father did have moments like this with me when I was very young, although their sublimity cannot be known: he sang much worse music with a much better voice. Is it more soul-stirring to massacre Mozart or to apply a true baritone to "They Call Me Little Good-for-Nothing"?

His work and his family were my father's whole life and they are my whole life as well, for my only pastimes are playing the piano, playing touch football, and bouncing checks; but in spite of his constant boyishness, in spite of his games of shot-for-shot and his whistling for cabs with two fingers in his mouth, my father was still too dignified to abandon himself to a child as I have abandoned myself to Lori. He was an athletic man of thirty-two when I was one year old, but he still never triggered laughter in me the way I trigger it in Lori by endlessly jumping over her head like a hurdler whose mind has started to slip; or by jogging around the block while pushing her stroller ahead of me; and of course it would have been unthinkable for my father to have played the scene that I played one morning when the telephone rang while Lori's bowel-rich diaper was at half-mast when my eldest daughter asked me to bring some clothing to her high school right away. As I held the diaper with one hand and made notes about pants and Peds with the other, I could hear my father say:

Poop, a real man doesn't live like this. If you had a job, you wouldn't be a chauffeur and a toilet at nine o'clock in the morning.

He never knew golden moments like these because the men of his generation were too mature to immerse themselves in their children with the kind of lunatic love that I have used as a substitute for employment. My father, of course, was not only employed, he was possessed. In fact, I ghosted one *Coronet* story for him entitled "I Married a Telephone" in which my mother was the added attraction in a bed that included my father and a phone. I have come to understand why both my sister and I were born in May. We had to be conceived on Labor Day, the only day of the year, as my father often said, when there was never any news.

Day and night, Paul Schoenstein was so involved in gathering the news that fathering was a sometime thing, a series of Sunday improvisations; but some of these improvisations make sweet replays in the theater of my mind. So, often I turn on mental tapes and return to places like a jeep that is touring Mitchell Field, where my father and I pretended we were generals reviewing the troops; like the deck of the battleship *New Jersey* anchored in the Hudson River, where we converted to admirals and tried to train our guns on the *New York Post;* and like the Polo Grounds, where I sat in a box with the former batboy of a Harlem team called the Lincoln Giants.

"I was the only white man on that team," my father told me one summer Sunday as we entered the Polo Grounds to see some other Giants play. As the only Caucasian on both the Lincoln Giants and the *Amsterdam News*, my father had undoubtedly been the city's most distinguished token white; and whenever our taxi passed through Harlem on our way to a game at the Polo Grounds, he would lose himself in happy recollection of those early days:

"A jig almost broke my jaw on that corner. What a punch he had . . . And over there, another one hit me with the top of a garbage can."

"Dammit, Poop, they're *Negroes*."

"I had fights with Negroes, too. But the jigs hit harder."

"You were a busy Jew bastard," I said.

Because my father had the attention span of a toddler for any activity that did not involve getting his newspaper to press, a day at the Polo Grounds with him was not a day in the mainstream of sport. My own attention was also split because my bladder was the most temporary of holding tanks and it was more important for me to know the way to the men's room than the names of the pitchers.

On the Sunday of that game, with the Giants playing the Brooklyn Dodgers, we had been in our seats for just a few minutes when my father turned to me and said what he said to me more often than any other words:

"Poop, do you need anything?"

All I ever wanted at a ball game was not to be in the men's room during a grand-slam home run; and my father was always so eager to please me that I would not have been surprised if he had somehow found a vender who was hawking latrines.

My trips to the men's room became counterpoint to my father's trips to visit friends, so that finding the two of us in the box together was as rare as the Giants not blowing a lead.

"Hey, there's Wally Bird," he said, spotting a famous movie actor whose name was similar to that. "Come on, we'll go over and say hello."

"Poop, I met him at the Inner Circle—and it's bases loaded," I said. "I think I'll stay here and watch a little of the game."

"Sure, whatever you want. But he'd get a big kick out of meeting you."

"I think you got it backwards. People are supposed to get a big kick out of meeting *him*. Poop, you gotta stop thinking that everybody wants to *meet* me. I mean, I never really found *one* who did—oh my God, that just curved foul!"

"Righto, Poop," said my father, not having listened to a word. "I'll give him your best. He's a very sweet guy and he'll be asking for you."

And off he went to Wally Bird, who should have been coming to my father bearing frankincense and myrrh. A few months earlier, Bird had found something that gave him an even bigger kick than meeting me: he had been a supporting player in a whorehouse when the police had made a raid and picked him up along with the staff. In panic, he had called my father and said that the publication of his name in this story would be the end of his career, for those were the days before lechery became the crowd pleaser it is today. Touched by Bird's entreaty, my father not only kept the story out of the *Journal-American* but he called the City Editors of the *World-Telegram*, the *Sun,* the *Mirror,* and the *News* and convinced them that they should kill it, too. The *Times,* of course, required no call: it had limited coverage of the whorehouse scene.

"If a cathouse story got out to his fans, the poor guy would be through," my father had told the City Editor of the *World-Telegram*, Lee Wood. "We'd better stick to reviewing his performances on the screen."

"Paul, are you calling Dolly Schiff, too?" Lee Wood had said.

"I don't have to," my father had replied. "No news ever gets to her anyway."

When my father returned from seeing Wally Bird, he carried a hot dog, a Giants pennant, and a Giants cap for me. If there is one picture of this man that will always shine in my memory, even brighter than the picture of his tearing up a summons or impersonating a cop, it is seeing him coming to me with gifts. His bounty is a standard that has become a part of me, for I can never buy a gift for one of my daughters, not a bracelet, a record, or even a joke, without wondering if my father would have bought a better one.

Why didn't you get that Snoopy T-shirt in Brooks Brothers? I hear him say.

After I had thanked him for the gifts and pretended I had wanted a tasteless hot dog, we sat together for a few moments and then he said, "What a terrific game. I've really enjoyed coming here with you, Poop."

His premature nostalgia had begun, his delight in reminiscing about an event that was still ahead of him. This Einsteinian ability to bend time, to sentimentally look back on the future, often made my father oblivious to the reality of the moment at hand; and even when he slipped into the present, he was sometimes charmingly unaware of what the hell was going on.

"What happened, Poop?" I once asked him as he drove up to our house at the beach with a dent in his car.

"The Lincoln Tunnel," he said. "Something hit me."

Since it was almost impossible for a car to be sideswiped in this tunnel where no passing was allowed, I could only say, "You mean . . . the *tunnel* hit you?"

"That must have been it," he replied, creating in me the same kind of awe that would have been felt by a desert observer if the mountain indeed had come to Mohammed.

In our box at the Polo Grounds, he was looking again at his watch when a voice called out, "Hey, Paul!"

It was Rabbit Maranville, the Hall of Fame shortstop of the Boston Braves, who now was writing a baseball column for the *Journal-American,* where many of his fellow columnists also had an infielder's prose style.

"Rabbit!" cried my father, shooting out his arm in the fascist salute that he always gave when overreacting to the sight of friends. "The best sports writer in town! Come over here and meet Ralph."

Once again, my father had it backwards, feeling that the man from the Hall of Fame would be thrilled to meet the child with mustard on his nose. However, when Maranville entered our box, my father regained his perspective and said, "Ralph, meet the greatest shortstop in the history of the game."

"And meet the greatest City Editor in the whole United States," said Maranville to me.

"Whose son is the greatest man in the world," my father said.

It was beginning to feel like a convocation of fertilizer

salesmen. The aroma was one that I knew well, for hyperbole had been the air I breathed. In the manner of William Randolph Hearst, Paul Schoenstein looked at life as a series of banner headlines; and I was so infected by this Hearstian view of things that I have never since felt comfortable with a moderate tone.

"I have the worst case of indigestion in recorded history," I once said to my wife, the only kind of gas that was fitting for the greatest man in the world.

After Maranville had left us, my father divided his time between looking at the game and at his watch, neither of which interested him as much as the makeup of Monday's first edition. As the fifth inning began, he got up and said, "I'm calling the office. Do you want anything?"

"I'll go with you," I said. "The phone's right next to the men's room."

The two of us were getting more exercise than most of the Giant hitters that day. At last, at the end of the eighth, he stood up and said, "We'd better go now, Poop, so we can beat the crowds."

And we beat them easily: not another person was leaving the park, because the Dodger pitcher, Rex Barney, had been throwing a no-hitter.

I was used to seeing such partial games with the peripatetic Paul Schoenstein. In fact, my clearest memory of our Sundays at the Polo Grounds and Yankee Stadium is mounting the stairs of the elevated train backwards, backing into one of the cars, and then jumping up on a seat, straining all the way to see the upper parts of home runs.

And on the following day I was careful to conceal from all my friends that, during the unassisted triple play in the bottom of the ninth, I was fiercely rooting from the Harlem River tunnel.

Rex Barney completed his no-hitter a few minutes after my father had begun to reminisce about it; and then he reminisced about the men's room.

"Did you have a reserved seat in there?" he said with a smile.

"Very funny," I said uneasily.

"Poop, you do make an awful lot of trips."

"Okay, I know."

"Well, maybe you could toughen up those kidneys a bit. One of these days, you'll have to be a man."

"Now how the hell do you toughen up *kidneys?*" I said. "And don't tell me *you* did it by getting yourself beat up in Harlem."

Our talks about anything urinogenital always made me squirm, although such talks were fleeting indeed. In spite of the closeness that we had, there still were certain subjects we did not plumb to the depths, and the biggest of these were sex and death. Sex he decided to save until I was thirty-five years old, but death he handled in a straightforward way.

"I'm Superman," he constantly said.

And so, as a child of the forties, I was hearing my father telling me that he could be killed only by material from the planet Krypton. Moreover, since I also knew that there *was* no planet Krypton, I was the only boy in America who never feared his father's death. A boy was lucky to have a father who shoveled shit so thoughtfully.

When we got home from a Sunday game, he began making phone calls to organize his first Monday edition and then we sometimes stripped down to our underwear, stretched out together on his double bed, and turned on the radio, a pastime he preferred to watching baseball games because the radio could be enjoyed while ignoring it for the telephone, the tabloids, or sleep. And I preferred it, too, for the wonderful thing about listening with him was that his own life supplemented the programs and gave their fantasies a bridge to reality that was never crossed by the boys whose fathers sold cat food or drilled into teeth.

For example, "Gangbusters" always opened with a burst of machine-gun fire, but the end of the show was more dramatic for me: the former head of the New Jersey State Police came on the air and moved my father to tell him off.

"You bubblehead," my father would say to the Philco that sat beside his bed.

"You really *know* Colonel Schwarzkopf?" I would ask him for the ninth or eighteenth time.

"I wish I didn't," he would reply. "I had a lot of trouble with him. He was certainly no help to me in the Lindbergh case."

Nobody was much help to my father in the Lindbergh case and that was why he didn't solve it; but even in those early days at the *Journal,* he was already reaching out for what he liked to call "a big one."

When "The F.B.I. in Peace and War" came on, I went into a similar litany.

"You really know the guys who run the F.B.I.?" I would ask him, tingling from the glamour that was electrifying the room where the two of us lay in our boxer shorts, my father looking like a heavyweight champion with his great hairy chest and I looking like a vision of Famine with the bones that connected my stomach and chin.

"I know Lou Nichols and Clyde Tolson better than I know you," he would say, making me wonder again about the quality of our relationship. Had he ever said to Nichols or Tolson, "I wish I knew my son as well as I know you"?

My father was also connected to less momentous shows like "Uncle Don," a man who read the *Journal-American* comics on the air to children he called his nephews and nieces. Uncle Don drank, an understandable avocation for anyone who had to read the *Journal-American* out loud.

"And now, for all my nephews and nieces, let's see what's doing in Puck the Comic Weekly," he used to say, a line that always sounded like "Fuck the Comic Weekly" to me. I was tempted to ask my father why his paper used a slogan that sounded like one of the walls in my school, but our relationship did not allow me to mention this word that he had learned when he was six.

One of Uncle Don's daily games was announcing the names of the children who were having birthdays and then giving a few of them clues about where their parents had hidden birthday gifts. Because of my father's influence at WOR, he was able to arrange for Uncle Don to give me annual messages like this: "And a happy eighth birthday to Ralphie Schoenstein of Manhattan, whose daddy prints all our wonderful comics. Ralphie, if you look in a bureau in one of the bedrooms that isn't your own, you're gonna find a big surprise." The year that he gave this particular clue, I found both my present and a big surprise as well: a bottle of gin in my father's shorts.

Uncle Don caused this kind of treasure hunting all over New York. In fact, the year before I found the gin, Freddie Cohen had celebrated his birthday by finding his mother's diaphragm; but he did not know what it was, even though he had written the decadent ditty that led our schoolyard hit parade:

> *My Bonnie lies over the ocean,*
> *My Bonnie lies over the sea.*
> *My mother lied over my father,*
> *And that's how I came to be.*

My father would have corrected the grammar of this little song but not the notion that mothers were generally on the top in the launching of new life. He was always so careful to protect me from the nasty business of sex that when Kinsey's *Sexual Behavior in the Human Male* came out, even though I was officially of age to masturbate, my father hid the book behind *Mein Kampf* and *The Collected Writings of William Randolph Hearst,* the only two unreadable books on our shelves.

No radio star could move my father to sharper retort than Walter Winchell, who came on Sunday nights at nine to report on how well he was running the world.

"Good evening, Mr. and Mrs. North and South America and all the ships at sea!" this transcendental egotist would cry and my father would once again reply, "Good evening, you son of a bitch," and then repeat the reason for his wrath: Winchell's failure to mention my birth in his column, which was printed in papers from coast to coast. My father felt that my arrival, while perhaps not quite as big a story as the arrival of the Dionne quintuplets, nevertheless deserved national coverage. He nurtured his anger at Winchell for thirty-one years; and then his chance for revenge finally came. The *Daily Mirror* folded and Winchell's column was moved to the *Journal*, where my father cut it in half almost every day, thus providing a public service because I had been insufficiently announced.

My father often talked from the other side of the radio too, for he had a persuasive and neutral voice that contained no trace of the streets where he had sold papers, rolled dice, and carried my mother's books home from her school. His voice, in fact, was so good that he once derailed a show called "Where Are You From?," which was run by a night-school Professor Higgins who tried to place people geographically by hearing them speak a few special words.

After my father had read such sentences as "Further and further went Foster's father" and "Mary married merry

Murray," the professor triumphantly announced that he was from eastern Iowa.

"Not quite," said my father with a grin. "I'm from western Harlem."

"But . . . you didn't spend your *entire* boyhood there," said the flustered professor.

"Oh, no," my father said.

"That's what I thought."

"I spent the rest of it in the Bronx."

The studio audience exploded with laughter while the professor tried to save face by saying, "Mr. Schoenstein, will you read that last sentence again?"

"Mary married merry Murray," said my father, "which is old news, I'm afraid. Why don't we give some baseball scores?"

In his many years as a happy ham, my father was a frequent guest on such shows as "We the People" and "Vox Pop"; but the highlight of his radio career, even brighter than his rigging of "Ellery Queen," was his singing of "The Anniversary Song" on a husband-and-wife show called "Tex and Jinx." He did it in a duet with a new young actor named David Wayne; and from that moment on, "The Anniversary Song" was his theme and opinon was split on his performing it. Those who disliked the song didn't want him to sing it and those who liked it felt the same way. However, many people felt that his joy in singing the song to my mother more than made up for his inability to remember the words that followed line one.

"Two hearts softly singing were loving so low," he sang at one party, and "Two hearts softly loving were beating so low," he sang at another. But in spite of the coronary damage that he inflicted on the song, the people who loved him always smiled warmly as he fought his way through it with the passion and ineptness of a six-year-old saying the Pledge of Allegiance.

From time to time, he added me to his act and we went on the air as father and son. Since my voice didn't change until I was sixteen, father and daughter was more our sound; but mercifully for the listeners, my father rarely let me speak. He would hold forth alone for a while and then say, "Ralph, how does *your* generation feel about that?"

"Well, Dad," I would reply in squeaky solemnity, "my friends and I feel—"

"Because it's important for those of us who shape the news to have our fingers on the pulse of America's youth," he would say, once again putting his hand not on the news or the pulse but right over my mouth.

On one program that we did, he and a hostess named Barbara Welles talked twenty-seven minutes and then she said, "I see you have a son with you today," as if I were a Pekinese.

"Yes, and he's quite a young man," my father said. "I think we should get his point of view."

"Which we'll have to do one day very soon," said Barbara Welles with a glance at the clock; and once again the Harpo Marx of father-and-son radio silently nibbled on his nails.

Because I had done some radio acting at Stuyvesant High School, generally playing the parts of women in the wonderful works of Norman Corwin, I felt that my father and I should have had a radio show of our own.

"We could call it 'What's the Poop, Poop?' " I told him one day. "Unless that would make too many people think of baby shit. Yeah, it would; we'd better call it something like 'Breakfast with Paul and Ralph.' Hey, we could even start off with the sound of you squeezing my orange juice and I could say, 'Thanks, Dad. And now what's juicy in the paper?' "

With enthusiasm like this, I convinced him to sit for a while with me and make a demonstration reel that we could send to WOR, where we could be used as either an appetizer or a chaser for "Breakfast with Dorothy and Dick." With the microphone of our wire recorder mounted on a Kleenex box, we sat ourselves at the kitchen table and looked at the world from two points of view: his and what he thought was mine. Of course, I had done such broadcasts before and so I should not have been surprised to have half of my sentences rendered incomplete by the man who never needed a partner to have a conversation.

The final radio connection between my father and me came on a night in my sophomore year at Hamilton College, when I made my three roommates hear "The Big Story" dramatize my father's exposé of a Harlem numbers ring for which he had probably worked as a boy. At nine o'clock, I proudly turned on the radio in our room and the four of us sat on our beds to hear:

NARRATOR (*solemnly*): Tonight the Big Story salutes . . . a fighting City Editor who rolled up his sleeves and took on the mob . . .

Music: Stirringly up and then under, as if announcing the invasion of Guadalcanal.

NARRATOR (*still talking to posterity*): It all began one afternoon at the *New York Journal-American,* when crack City Editor Paul Schoenstein, already the holder of the Pulitzer Prize, called three of his ace reporters to his desk and said . . .

SCHOENSTEIN: Men, there's a lot of vice in Harlem and I want to get rid of it. Can do?

AN ACE REPORTER: Can do, boss.

SCHOENSTEIN: We'll go undercover on this one.

ANOTHER ACE REPORTER: Check, boss.

SCHOENSTEIN: Tommy, I want you to pose as a telephone-repair man. Harry, you set up a shoeshine stand. And, Al, you're a tourist from Buffalo.

THE THIRD ACE: Good thinking, boss.

SCHOENSTEIN: I'm after more than just the numbers racket, boys. I want prostitution, dope, hijacking—the works. And I want plenty of names and addresses, so we can turn the story right over to the D.A. But be careful. Don't let 'em know who you are. Remember how I lost Syd Boehm when the Nazis found out he was working for me.

The show continued in this tone for another thirty minutes while I sat on my bed and wished I were listening to "Young Widder Brown." I kept waiting for my father to go into a phone booth and change to his cape and tights. When the purple half hour was finally over, when my father had told the police where they could pick up Harlem's leading racketeers, there was silence in my room while my roommates tried to find some words.

At last, a boy named Sam White said, "That was nice, the way your old man cleaned up Harlem—yeah, it was nice."

"Well, not *all* of Harlem," I modestly replied. "And even what he cleaned up got a little dirty again. That show was a bit melodramatic, you know."

"Yeah, a bit, I guess," he said.

There was silence again and I was about to discuss our history test when a boy named Herbie Glassman suddenly jumped to his feet and solemnly said, "Men, there's a lot of pussy out there and I want you to clean it up. We'll go undercover tonight—two of you, that is. Schloimey, you go under the bed. But if you have to come out for any reason, for God's sake don't let 'em know that you're white. You remember how Freddie the Fink almost lost his balls when the Dragon Lady found out he was from the *Journal-American.* And if you need any help in spotting a pussy, just let me know. That's why they call me Crack."

While Herbie was doing his parody, I felt angry, embarrassed, and amused, three moods that rarely come at once unless your father is a Hearst editor who had made you vulnerable again.

"For *Crissake,* Herbie," said Sam, "what's *wrong* with you? That's his *father,* you jerk!"

"*He* knows I'm just kidding," Herbie said. "Hell, a program about your old man is *great.* The only program *my* old man could get would be a police call."

"I think it's a wonderful honor," Sam told me, "even if your father does work for Hearst."

"Oh, my father doesn't work for Hearst," I said. "He plays the piano in a whorehouse."

All of us laughed and I seized the opportunity to start talking about the Treaty of Versailles. I was seventeen years old and that bawdy piano was still playing for me. Its music, however, had become as natural as the air I breathed. I didn't know then, of course, that when this music finally stopped, the silence would be almost too much to bear.

7

POOP AND GUTS

The camp was called Wigwam and it was a place in Maine where chic Jewish boys hid from polio germs during the summers I love to recall. It had been my destiny to go there, of course, because under the law of generational contrasts that governed my boyhood, my father's father hadn't sent him to camp.

"Father never wanted me to miss the New York Summer Festival," my father said, "with its wonderful opportunities to have your teeth removed."

Richard Rodgers, J. D. Salinger, and Frank Loesser had gone to Wigwam before me, but none of them had been captured by a *Journal-American* photographer, who followed me through Grand Central Station on that steamy noisy night in 1945 as if he were doing a photo essay on obscure people of twelve. One of the pictures that he took, part of my father's running coverage of that non-event known as my youth, appeared in the July 1 *Journal-American* over the caption SUMMER EXODUS; and exodus was a fitting word, for there was a refugee tone to the shot.

I stood beside an inverted canoe paddle that looked like a model of my chest and it was hard to tell whether I was supporting the paddle or the paddle was supporting me. My white shirt billowed like a sail in the breeze and my mouth had a melancholy smile that allowed my braces to sparkle from the light of the Hearst flashbulb.

"I'd like this camp to put a little meat on your bones," my father said on that night at Grand Central as he slipped me a twenty-dollar bill. "And I want you to use this experience to try to really be a man. Of course, if there's anything you need, you know that all you have to do is pick up a phone."

My father's advice always had an option for ignoring it. Paul Schoenstein was a man who would send you money to make you self-reliant and who would call you long-distance three times a week to remind you to be tough.

An hour after he had given me a soggy goodbye kiss, I was lying in a lower berth as the train flew over the Harlem streets, where boys were still playing stickball even though dusk was turning to night. They were straining to pick up their spaldeens in the vanishing city light the way I had done for years on streets without the hunks of glass; and I knew they were hoping that first base or third wouldn't suddenly drive away. Watching them made me think of my father, who had spent his summers romping and stealing on these same Harlem streets, while trainloads of middle-class babies went by on their way to be toughened in New Hampshire and Maine.

At Camp Wigwam, I was introduced to a version of

stickball that was called baseball and I decided that I wanted to make junior varsity at second base. This was the ideal position to play for a boy with my special athletic skills: a weak throwing arm and a fear of ground balls. I needed a spot in the infield where the softest grounders were hit; and I needed a spot no more than ten or fifteen feet from first base, in case the ball found its way to my glove like a magnetic torpedo seeking out a ship that was maneuvering to let it pass by.

In the first games of baseball that I played, sometimes with a quickly scrawled note and a five-dollar bill from my father in my pants, I had amazingly few errors for a fielder so inept, because I often moved far enough from the ball to allow it to be a clean base hit. As I stood in the field and prayed for the batter to hit the ball to someone else, I could hear my father saying, *Come on, Poop, keep your head down and open your eyes;* and I could hear my Wigwam baseball coach, Eddie "Rah Rah" Rose, saying, "Well, maybe you'll do better at bat."

At bat, however, avoidance was also the key to my playing style. Because I was so short, I decided not to swing at any balls that summer but instead to work the pitchers for walks. My grand design, therefore, was to be a junior-varsity second baseman who never touched the ball with his glove or his bat.

"Ralphie, I like your spirit and your speed," Rah Rah told me at practice one day, "but sooner or later you're gonna have to get involved with the ball."

"I'm never very far from it," I said.

"Look, Ralphie, I know you're afraid of the ball, so you're just gonna have to dig in there and have guts. When you're out in the field, I want you to force yourself to keep facing the plate. And when you're at bat, I want you to stand up and face the pitcher like a man."

"But with my height—and the way I crouch," I said, "I'm a cinch to walk almost every time."

I did have a point. My crouch at the plate was so severe that I looked like someone who was about to be spanked.

"No, I don't want you to go through the summer like a midget with cramps," Rah Rah Rose said. "I want you to show your stomach. In other words, Ralphie, show your guts."

After giving me this speech in different forms a couple of times, Rah Rah began to call me "Guts," and so did the other boys on the team, though some of them seemed less than sincere.

"Are you Guts or Putz—I forget," said a boy named Roger Rappaport.

The challenge that I faced in this summer of '45 now was clear to me. If I wanted to prove myself a man to my father and Rah Rah and all the boys, I would have to do more than stop wetting the bed, although that would have been a good opening move. I would also have to charge a ball that was slammed toward second base and let it hit me in the face. Maybe it would even move my orthodontia along.

As the second-string second baseman on Wigwam's junior varsity team, I appeared in four games by July 17, walking five times, striking out twice, and three times getting hit by the pitch. The third time, when a ball caught me on that fine line known as my chest, I loved the pain more than Masoch himself and I said to Rah Rah elatedly, "You *see?* I can do more than just *walk:* I can get myself *hit.* And you don't hear a *whimper* out of me."

"Listen, Guts," said Rah Rah with a sympathetic grin, "you may be built like a bat but you gotta start hitting the ball with something else. I mean, I like your spunk, but *Blood* and Guts is another guy."

On July 20, I sat amid the comic books on the bed in my bunk and wrote:

Dear Mom and Dad:

Camp is still really great! I haven't wet the bed *one* time and I've stopped saying "swell" so much and I've played in *four* junior varsity games.

Poop, you'd really be proud of me because everybody calls me Guts. That's because I go after the ball with a lot more than my bat. There'll be a father-son game on Parents Weekend and I can't wait because you'll get a chance to see me play and *you* can play *too!* Tell Rabbit Maranville I'm really learning how to pivot on the double play and I hope to make one before the summer is over.

Love,
Guts

A few days later, a big envelope came to me from the *Journal-American.* It not only contained a typical six-line letter from my father, giving a brief description of the weather and World War II, but it also contained a stirring drawing by the paper's best artist, Burris Jenkins, Jr. He had drawn two faces side-by-side: one was Douglas Mac-Arthur, looking like a head on Mount Rushmore, and the other was Ralph Schoenstein, wearing an Army hat and looking like a head on Halloween. Underneath these two grim faces, these fighting sons of Hearst, Jenkins had written:

MAC AND GUTS

They shall return!

It hardly would have been bravado for me to have said that I would return, because the scheduled closing date of Camp Wigwam had long been known; but my father had been so impressed by my new nickname that he had gone into a Hearstian collaboration with Jenkins and produced the kind of astigmatic view of truth that had created the career of Marion Davies and the Spanish-American War.

Now, as Parents Weekend approached, I knew I would have to play second base with exceptional fortitude, charging to my left as well as to my right. In fact, I preferred going to my left because it took me even closer to first.

On the first Saturday of August, the big weekend began as parents arrived to meet counselors and exchange gratuities and lies. When my father arrived, he brought a carton of Hershey bars and a carton of Baby Ruths as if he were liberating an Italian town; and as I gleefully ran to him, a boy with short pants on his bony legs, we looked like a scene in which I should have been offering him my sister. This military image was heightened by a colonel who accompanied my parents that day, a thickly muscled and bouncy man in his early forties named Mickey Marcus. A former West Point boxing champion, he would soon leave on a secret mission to Palestine to help create an army for Israel, and on the night of the truce that ended the War of Independence, he would become its final casualty, accidentally killed by an Israeli sentry. With arms even stronger than my father's and an oil drum of a chest, Marcus exuded so much strength that he made my other Army associate, Douglas MacArthur, look like a commander from Abercrombie and Fitch.

As I walked across the campus toward my bunk with these two men, enjoying the glow of reflected virility, a boy who was passing said, "Hi-ya, Guts."

"That's what they call Ralph," said my father to Mickey with a smile of pride.

"A very fine name," Mickey told me. "Our commander on Guadalcanal was called Guts. And of course there's General Patton, too."

"Oh, those guys, they're *really* Guts," I said. "I'm small intestines compared to *them.*"

Mickey laughed. "Very good. Did you just think that up?"

Because he was a West Pointer, I had to say, "No, I thought of it last week. But this is the first time I've used it—*honest.* I made up another one, too. You know what the weather report will be on the day that we hang Tojo?"

"No, what?"

"There's a Nip in the air."

He laughed again and said, "Paul, how did a bum like you ever get a kid like this?"

"He's gonna be President," my father replied.

"Guts, you have a wonderful mind."

"Thanks, colonel," I told him. "I try to keep it in shape. I think I got the nickname for the wrong part of me."

"How did you get it?" he said.

I couldn't make myself reply, *I learned not to run away from the ball,* so I said, "Gee, I really forget." And then I quickly said to my father, "Hey, Poop, are you ready for the big game tomorrow?"

"You bet," he said as we approached my bunk.

"What position are you playing?"

"What do you *want* me to play?"

"Well, where did you play with the Lincoln Giants?"

"I was the guy who went for the beer."

"But you told me . . . I mean, I told the guys . . . well, *please* don't say anything about *that.*"

"Oh, he'll be DiMaggio for them," Mickey said. "You know that your father never tells a story the same way twice."

"Listen, Poop, when you meet my counselor . . . please go easy on how great I am. You're the only one who knows."

The following day, I was doubly nervous, worried about my own performance and also about the performance of the bartender of the Lincoln Giants. I had put out my usual Hearst press release about him to the other boys in the camp: that he was the youngest and strongest father in America, that he had been the only white man on a professional Negro team, and that he could hit a ball a mile. My father *could* hit a ball a mile, but only when he was playing tennis. Whenever we played Sunday tennis on a court on West End Avenue, he managed to put his awesome strength into at least one shot and send it toward the Hudson as a two-sewer forehand.

At two o'clock, the fathers and sons assembled on the baseball field and began warming up. Mickey Marcus, now in civilian clothes, was hitting ground balls to my father, who was swiping at them as if he were sweeping water from a leaky boat. It was, of course, hard for him to see any little objects approaching because of the smoke sent up by the cigarette that hung from his lips.

"Your old man thinks he's Humphrey Bogart?" Roger Rappaport said to me. "The Lincoln Giants were a prison team?"

"No, smoking relaxes him," I said, watching my father uneasily.

"He fields like Bogart. But I guess he's Guts, too, eh? Boy, Ralphie, they make 'em tough in your house. I bet your mother wears Army shoes."

"Up your ass with a malted machine," I said, revealing the command of language that would gain me admission to Stuyvesant High School when I returned from camp; and then I ran to my father and said, "Hey, Poop, *please* don't clown around. This is a *serious game*. I mean that *cigarette* . . ."

"Are you kidding?" he said. "You just be ready to handle what I hit you."

In no way reassured, I ran back to the campers' side of the field and continued to spit into my glove, which resembled a leather cuspidor. Any ball that arrived there might have floated right out, but the spitting was part of the style that I felt a boy with my nickname had to display. I could, of course, have kept my brave saliva to myself had I had the talent to live my fantasy of lining sharp singles to center field; but in those accidental moments when my bat intercepted the ball, my hands were left stinging from the feeble ground-out; and so I had to let my mouth be the most aggressive part of me. In addition to spitting on myself, I was also the cheerleader of the infield.

"Hum, babe! Hum, babe! Hum, babe!" I used to cry, a phrase that might have had some meaning in a choral competition but never did much to inspire my pitcher to keep the batter from hitting the ball through my legs.

There was, however, no cheerleader like Rah Rah, who now stood in front of our team and said, "I want you guys to go out there and show your old men what you're made of. Don't be soft on 'em just because they're paying the bills. I want you to give me a hundred and ten percent. And that extra ten percent . . ." He patted his stomach, which rose like an early pregnancy beneath a Yale T-shirt. "That'll come from *here*." And then he turned grimly to me. "Okay, Guts, let's start things off! Make some contact up there!"

Suddenly my mouth went dry. Someone else would have to spit on my glove; but when I walked up to the plate to be the campers' lead-off man, I switched to another show of style and rubbed some dirt into my hands, thus giving myself a better grip for striking out.

As I took my place in the batter's box, I looked at my father, who was smiling at me from shortstop, and I knew that he wanted to say, *Do you need anything, Poop? Would you like an intentional walk?* What I felt now was more complex than the feel of somebody shaving basketball points: I wanted to play well and courageously for a team that won while my father played well and smokelessly for one that lost.

In spite of what Rah Rah had told me about making contact with the ball, I instinctively sank into my crouch, eliminated my strike zone, and drew a walk. When I reached first base, my father smiled at me and with a sweep of his arm suggested that I come to second, once again as if calling a cab. I responded with a look that Ty Cobb might have made before trying to perforate a shortstop's legs. If the next batter, Fats Mandelbaum, moved me only as far as second base, there was a chance that my father might give me a hug or put some money into my uniform.

"Look alive, Guts!" Rah Rah cried. "No double play! Go in there hard!"

"Let's see ya put your father on his ass!" cried Roger Rappaport.

While I was looking at my father and wondering how I

could respectfully knock him down with a slide, Mickey
Marcus went running out to shortstop. He said a few words
to my father, who called time and started running toward
me.

My God, I thought. *It's a message from my mother to be
careful with my testicles.* I had a sensitive vein in the left
one and a doctor had told me to play carefully with it, a
suggestion I'd been dreaming of giving to a girl named
Gloria Strauss.

Mickey's message, however, concerned a matter more
cosmic than my loins.

"Poop, I've got a big one!" he said like a cub reporter of
forty-three. "We just dropped a helluva bomb on Japan—
ten thousand tons of TNT! I've gotta get to a phone!"

Exploding himself from the frustration of being three
hundred miles from the city room, he took off toward the
nearest telephone while a couple of people bent over the
radio that had given Mickey Marcus the news. A scrawny,
gray-haired man in Bermuda shorts took my father's place,
but I was too upset to think about a way to knock him
down, especially since he looked as though he might fall
down on his own. I was used to my father leaving ball
games early, but never with nine innings to go, and I felt
angry at losing a chance to prove my guts to him, perhaps
even with a belly slide that involved the left side of my
balls.

"Damn it," I said aloud, thus becoming the first American to curse the atomic age.

When would I get another chance to prove my guts to

him? Every time the two of us had put on boxing gloves, he turned the fight into a joke. He would let me hit him with all my might and then pretend nobody was there; and of course nobody was.

As I took a lead off first and watched Fats Mandelbaum get set to connect against a junk-balling CPA, I continued to think of my father and I knew without hearing a word what he was saying on the phone:

And tell Leo and Johnny I want all the scientific dope on exactly what this big bomb is . . . I don't care if it's a secret . . . Go with everything the AP has, but I also want a dramatic drawing of what the bomb would do to New York. You can have it landing on the Post *. . . Of course I'm coming right back. I just had to see Ralph play five minutes of ball . . . Oh yeah, he's sensational. Another Rabbit Maranville.*

8

UP, UP, AND AWAY

He must have been flabbergasted to find himself dead because Superman should not have been laid out in the Riverside Memorial Chapel; but during almost fifty years of never missing a day's work because of illness, he also had never stopped asking for lung cancer and his request had finally been granted.

CANCER CURE FOUND

was the headline of the newspaper he had helped me create as homework for a journalism class at Stuyvesant High.

"Would a cure for cancer be the biggest story ever?" I had asked him then.

"Pretty close to it," he had replied. "But I guess the very biggest story would be the Second Coming—or your mother's brother picking up a check."

Cheapness bothered my father as much as a room whose door was closed or a visit to a hospital or thirteen people sitting down to dine. It was only a few weeks before he died that I learned that he had cut up his Pulitzer Prize money and shared it with seven other men in the *Journal-American* city room, making him the first winner in the history of the prize to get sixty-two dollars and fifty cents.

I will always wonder if my father knew what was wrong with him at the end, for he lied so splendidly to others that he may have fallen under his own spell. He was a man who was able to tell you while he was pouring out a Scotch, "I've stopped my drinking, you know." And you would believe it.

As he entered the hospital for the last time, he said, "I don't want anyone to think that this is serious, especially the Hearst people. So when people call, Poop, you just tell 'em I'm having a little polyp removed."

The little polyp was his left lung; but in spite of his condition, he still was eager to return to the job he had been given when the *World Journal Tribune* went down: categorizing the papers of William Randolph Hearst. It has been said that every man is eloquent at least once in his life, but Mr. Hearst was a shining exception; and so my father's job was a challenge on the level of collecting the wit and wisdom of Henry Ford.

This job, nonetheless, became his only link to the Hearst organization. When I went to see him one December day in the Hearst Building on Eighth Avenue, where both his office and his body had shrunk from the size they had been when he was heavyweight champion of the *Journal* city room, he got up from a desk full of old newspapers and gave me an outline of an autobiography that he had been planning to write for twenty-five years, an outline that he had finally expanded to a half a page:

> *Mad Bomber*
> *City Editor*
> *Mr. New York*
> *Political Contacts*
> *How I Started*
> *Experience at University of California*
> *Categorizing All of Mr. Hearst's Papers*
> *My Salary as City Editor*

I was shocked to see that he had found his salary and his work on Hearst's papers worth mentioning, but he had left out the winning of the Pulitzer Prize, the capture of a German spy, the destruction of Harlem's biggest crime ring, the destruction of the New Jersey and Long Island Bunds, the exposure of Rockland State Hospital, the exposure of television's crooked quiz shows, and the story that helped to change the medieval divorce law in the state of New York.

His experience at the University of California, however, was a triumph that belonged on the list. After a year of odd jobs in San Francisco, he had enrolled at the university in a unique early-admissions program: skipping high school; and, as preparation for skipping high school, he also had skipped the eighth and seventh grades. Nevertheless, he had been doing well in his college freshman year until the dean asked for his high-school records. My father's story of a fire in the school was an amateurish response. Had the attempted expulsion involved a more mature Paul Schoenstein, one who already had finished his doctorate in the uses of the fix, the dean not only would have received a set of my father's high-school records but they would have been those of Woodrow Wilson.

"Poop, this would make a hell of a book," he told me that day in his cluttered little office while I tried not to keep noticing how thin his arms had become. He was finally ready to be taken at shot-for-shot.

"Absolutely," I said, "so why don't we write it. We could call it *Citizen Bullshit*. The story of a fighting City Editor —fighting his publisher, fighting his unions, fighting his son, who wants a column . . . In the movie, Charles Bronson could play you—as a boy, that is."

Without laughing, without even hearing me, he began to shake his head and say, "I just can't get over it. The goddam *Post* in the *Journal* building. At least Dolly Schiff doesn't have my old office."

"Look at it this way," I said. "Only a guy as tough as you was able to survive on that South Street food. I give them all six months to live."

"I've got a great responsibility here, you know," he said with a gesture to the Hearst outpouring that would have been worthless whether shaped by a librarian or an orangutan. "I've got to categorize all of this—and plenty more."

"Why not just categorize it as crap and then you're finished," I said; but I still was unable to make him smile.

At that moment, Jim Kilgallen, a father who had never

minded his daughter also working for Hearst, passed the open door and my father shot up his arm and cried, "Hey, Jim!"

"Hello, Paul," Kilgallen softly said.

My father had so few visitors here that he pounced on this stiff little white-haired man as if he were a stewardess bringing a drink.

"Jim, come on *in*. You remember Ralph."

And I suddenly thought: *Jim, I'm the man who would have gotten a TV column when Dorothy died if my father had fought for me the way he had fought on Lenox Avenue.*

A few minutes later, at a restaurant across the street, my father and I sat together and tried to think of things to say.

"Do you need any money?" he asked me.

"No, I'm fine," I said, lying so smoothly that he should have been proud of me.

After a lull in which he kept tapping his fingers and staring into space, he raised his right arm to a passing waiter and I expected him to say, "Waiter, you remember Ralph."

He ordered a vodka that the doctor had forbidden, while I kept searching for conversational leads. I had run out of talk about my work and his was too dreary to discuss. I finally fell back on a story about one of my daughters, to which he replied, "Do you need any money?"

He had never been much of a listener, but now he had drifted so far from me that if I had told him, "The IRS has just taken my house," he would have replied, "That's good, Poop. I always want you to take good care of Judy and the girls."

After lunch, when we left the restaurant, he was cold in spite of his winter coat and his once-springy step was very slow. I put my hand on his arm to support him, and as I did, my mind rejected this picture of us and sent me back to Christmas 1943. I could hear Bing Crosby singing "I'll Be Home for Christmas" while my father overtipped a man to drag an enormous tree into our house. I loved the arrival of this tree because it meant that I was about to have another typical Christmas of an American boy: lunch with Jimmy Walker at Toots Shor's, a hundred-dollar gift from F. A. O. Schwarz, a couple of Happy Hanukkah cards, a Christmas Eve party for two hundred people that I could crash in my pajamas, and a Christmas Day brunch at that cathedral of high society, the Stork Club.

The Stork Club: the pinnacle of Paul Schoenstein's climb. Toots Shor's was a West Side saloon and the men whose backs Shor slapped were sometimes as rumpled as a *Journal* reporter; but at the Stork Club, off Fifth Avenue, the laughter was soft, the collars were hard, and the next man through the door would not be a pitcher for the Red Sox but a possible prince of the Romanoffs.

When my father and I came through that door on Christmas Day of 1943, he in his impeccable pin-striped suit and I in my baggy checkered jacket with the bombardier's wings in the lapel, he gave our coats to a hat-check

girl and told her "Merry Christmas, dear" as if he had
known her all his life; and then he turned to a man in a
tuxedo who was standing beside a red velvet rope, the
dapper sentry who decided which people had acceptable
genes or jewels or jobs.

"Merry Christmas, Mr. Schoenstein," said the man in a
Hungarian accent.

"*Hudge vudge,* Henry," said my father, using half the
Hungarian he knew. "You remember Ralph."

Henry, of course, remembered me well, for how many
other ten-year-olds had come into the club at night and
taken the edge off the class by ordering a malted milk?

And then the red velvet rope fell the way my father
made ropes fall all over New York, from Radio City Music
Hall to Cardinal Spellman's home, and he led my mother,
my sister, and me along the Stork Club's mink-filled bar
until we reached the entrance to the Cub Room, the inner
ring of Paradise, where another black-jacketed gentleman
smiled and led us to a corner booth that had black ash
trays with tiny white storks. It was a rather baroque cere-
mony just to have a plate of eggs, but my father loved
every obsequious move, for now the kid from Lenox
Avenue was sitting with accents from London and Cannes.

A few minutes after we were seated, Sherman Billingsley
left the Maharajah of Baroda and came to see us. A boot-
legging Oklahoma ex-convict, Billingsley operated a club
that would not have admitted him. He gave my mother
and sister bottles of Chanel No. 5 and then said, "Paul,
you should give some of this to your copy girls," referring

to the replacements for the *Journal* copy boys, who had
gone to war.

"I should give them cyanide," said my father with a
smile. "Sherm, how do you get women not to cry?"

"When they work for you, I'm surprised the men aren't
crying, too," my mother said and everyone at the table
laughed.

"Crying is part of a woman's charm," said Billingsley.

"Not at press time," my father replied.

"Your Lonergan story was sensational, Paul."

"I almost cried at that one myself. We were on the
streets for two whole hours with his confession while
Hogan kept denying it. The old Boy Scout D.A. I've never
sweated one out like that."

"I guess you can't tell me how you got it."

"Syd Boehm can find out anything. Even how much you
underpay your waiters."

"Paul, you've got to do a book."

"I just returned an advance to Simon and Schuster. A
thousand bucks. I don't have the time to write a book."

"He's also illiterate," my mother said.

"That we all know," said Billingsley as a photographer
with breasts that seemed to have been in a pencil sharp-
ener came by to capture our Christmas fun.

"Could you use her, Paul?" said Billingsley.

"She could cry through all five editions," my father said.

After that brunch, I went home to play with a big
metal model of a B-24 that my father had recently given
to me; and he had promised to take me flying in one

because "I know Jimmy Doolittle better than I know you."
I never got that ride and my father must have resented
the Air Corps wasting the plane on beating the Axis instead of taking us up for a Sunday spin above New York
so he could point to the skyline and say, "Well, Poop,
there it is. The town that I've put on the map."

He would have hated the obituary that I wrote for him
because it was both anonymous and for *The New York
Times.*

"If they won't run it with your byline," he would have
said, "freelance it somewhere else."

I wrote it while sitting on the edge of the bathtub in
his suite at Mount Sinai Hospital, while he talked on the
phone to a Hearst official who had one last favor to ask
of him: find Randolph Hearst's missing daughter, Patricia.
It was my father's kind of assignment, for if anyone could
have found her, it would have been the man with the
million contacts and the sixth sense, the man who would
have had a reporter take Mary Magdalene to a hotel for
a week, the man who saw the *Hindenburg* passing the
Journal and said aloud, "That thing is gonna crash."

He never liked letting anyone down; and when I saw
him at the funeral home, I could hear him saying, "I'm
working on this Patty Hearst thing now, Poop, so don't
tell the Hearst people that I'm dead."

In all the forty-one years that I knew him, he never
dropped his Superman pose to reveal a sense of mortality
to me; but he revealed it to my mother in a letter he

wrote one night from the city room of the old *Evening Journal* in October of 1929, just a week before he was married.

Saturday – Eight bells
At the uptown office . . .

My only love,

A million, billion, trillion apologies. I've been trying to write to you ever since I spoke to you on Thursday. Can you imagine my not writing to the only one in the world I care for and the only one I am thinking of?

But blame it all on sleep. Last night I sat me down—or almost did—to the typewriter to be interrupted by the worst catastrophe that ever hit New York, as you will note from the enclosed clipping.

Dearest, it was appalling; the town was in an uproar; everywhere pandemonium reigned. Poor devils bound for home, for the theatre, to be caught in the trap of death; to meet horrible, instantaneous death like rats. Men, women, and children swept to doom without a chance to fight.

And inside of every newspaper office there also was a wave of excitement. Those that were drunk—and there were many, as usual—found the tragedy had a sobering effect. Everyone uses the subways. And the word on everyone's tongue was: "Christ, I might have been in that train."

You know, dearest, it takes a catastrophe such as this to bring home the point that we never know when and where and how we're going to be bumped into oblivion. So let's live while we live; let's be happy; and don't let petty things cast a pall on our lives.

I adore you.

Paul

Although he has finally been bumped into oblivion himself, although the *Journal-American,* the Polo Grounds, the

Stork Club, and so many other places we knew have been relocated in oblivion too, I am reminded of him by something almost every day of my life: when I exaggerate for dramatic effect, when I picture myself in bed with my daughter's teacher or my dentist's nurse, when I pick up a phone just to have a few laughs with a friend in Anchorage, when my mind tunes out of a conversation and tunes in to my work, when I overtip a taxi driver or delivery boy, when I reach for a challenge to prove my guts, when I give another telephone operator a lesson in how to pronounce my name, and when I am so anxious to please my wife or one of my daughters that I seem more like a Japanese waiter than a husband and father to them. I start each day by going to a crib and lifting out my smallest girl, who offers me her lips for the kind of soggy kiss my father gave and points her finger at me the way he pointed his finger at Jimmy Walker while explaining how New York should be run.

His journalistic style seems so definitive to me that I stupidly resent the newspapermen who have followed him. Whenever I travel in America, I find myself drawn against my will to wander into city rooms and the visits are melancholy ones because these places don't seem real and their people are all impostors to me. In one of them last year, a coldly gleaming city room in St. Paul, I walked about with eyes that were seeing the *Journal-American*'s sixth floor. The windows I was seeing had grime that had started to form when the *Hindenburg* went by and the walls were losing paint that had been applied when the

Normandie went down. The only clean thing in that room was the Brooks Brothers shirt on the City Editor, the former Harlem newsboy who was quickly remaking page one, only minutes before press time, because he had landed another big one.